SAGE was founded in 1965 by Sara Miller McCune to support the dissemination of usable knowledge by publishing innovative and high-quality research and teaching content. Today, we publish over 900 journals, including those of more than 400 learned societies, more than 800 new books per year, and a growing range of library products including archives, data, case studies, reports, and video. SAGE remains majority-owned by our founder, and after Sara's lifetime will become owned by a charitable trust that secures our continued independence.

Los Angeles | London | New Delhi | Singapore | Washington DC | Melbourne

Advance Praise

'WHAT? Another leadership book?', you may ask. Yes, and this one is different. Jónsson and de Waal, practitioners not theoreticians, see leadership/followership experiences through both pragmatic and neurological 'lenses', simplifying both complexities and daily applications. This is neither a textbook nor a cookbook, but a set of down-to-earth explanations of what so often goes wrong and how to get them right going forward. Highly recommended!

Dr Steve F. Foster
Organisational Psychologist and Management Educator

Leadership is not just about leading or managing a group of people; it is rather a skill that brings together many qualities such as to set a right vision to encourage and inspire people to proactively work with that vision to coach and build the team to achieve success as a team and as an individual. This book brings together all these elements immaculately. It is, therefore, highly recommended.

Dr Satarupa Bhattacharjee Kapoor
CEO, Pristdel

A must-read for today's leaders. The book offers insights into effective leadership and develops leaders not only to steer organisations during the present time but also to brace the future. By applying Whole Brain Thinking, the authors have launched a contemporary management guidebook for the leaders of today and tomorrow.

Arvind Sinha
CEO, SAS Motors Limited

Finally, a book that brings all the strands for the personal and professional journeys to effective leadership into focus like never before! The Whole Brain Leader is not only a book for our times, but it is also a roadmap for all times, crystallising everything you need to best serve your organisation in extraordinary clarity.

Adam Honey
Founder and CEO, Sky Events,
Mountain Leap Events and Chamonix Ski Chalets

This book is a must-read for all. Ingvar Jónsson and Sjoerd de Waal have done a great job in explaining the 'VUCA' approach. The book takes a practical and easy-to-read path to solve most of the problems that a leader faces. Every business leader must apply Whole Brain thinking and use the suggested tools to effectively transform their business leadership.

Joydeep Bhattacharya
Digital Marketing Analyst

This book will help you tread the path of success by utilising your complete potential. It is easy to assimilate, imbibe and follow. It will create a lasting impression on your personal and professional lives.

Mayank Kumar
CEO, eVanik

'Disruption is all around us … for leadership this means change'. Jónsson and de Waal manage to create a complete toolbox for the modern leader. Their VUCA approach captures the complexity and speed of change of our times and, at the same time, the whole brain methodology provides a complete platform for continuous transformation. A must-read for any serious leader!

Dr Chrisoula Papadopoulou
Head of Department of Business and Management,
Webster University

Understanding people's behaviour, needs, drives and desires is, according to me, the essence of true leadership. This book is very accessible and introduces hands-on-tools that can help you grow to become an even more successful leader—it's a whole brainer!

Bogi Þór Siguroddsson
Author,
Entrepreneur and Strategic Leader

We are living in challenging times, and we need to use all our resources optimally. Managers of today need to be superheroes in order to succeed in this dynamic business environment, and this book will help you become one! It will help you become a true leader who builds further leadership as a continuous process. You will not just inspire yourself, you will inspire others to lead.

Kapil Rampal
Entrepreneur, Managing
Director of Ivory Education Pvt Ltd

THE WHOLE BRAIN LEADER

THE WHOLE BRAIN LEADER

8-DIMENSIONAL APPROACH

**INGVAR JÓNSSON
SJOERD DE WAAL**

Los Angeles | London | New Delhi
Singapore | Washington DC | Melbourne

Copyright © Ingvar Jónsson and Sjoerd de Waal, 2018

All rights reserved. No part of this book may be reproduced or utilised in any form or by any means, electronic or mechanical, including photocopying, recording, or by any information storage or retrieval system, without permission in writing from the publisher.

First published in 2018 by

SAGE Publications India Pvt Ltd
B1/I-1 Mohan Cooperative Industrial Area
Mathura Road, New Delhi 110 044, India
www.sagepub.in

SAGE Publications Inc
2455 Teller Road
Thousand Oaks, California 91320, USA

SAGE Publications Ltd
1 Oliver's Yard, 55 City Road
London EC1Y 1SP, United Kingdom

SAGE Publications Asia-Pacific Pte Ltd
3 Church Street
#10-04 Samsung Hub
Singapore 049483

Published by Vivek Mehra for SAGE Publications India Pvt Ltd, typeset in 10.5/14 pts Archer by Zaza Eunice, Hosur, Tamil Nadu, India and printed at Chaman Enterprises, New Delhi.

Library of Congress Cataloging-in-Publication Data

Names: Jónsson, Ingvar, author. | de Waal, Sjoerd, author.
Title: The whole brain leader : 8-dimensional approach / by Ingvar Jónsson and Sjoerd de Waal.
Description: Thousand Oaks, CA : SAGE Publications India Pvt Ltd, [2018] | Includes bibliographical references.
Identifiers: LCCN 2017053031 (print) | LCCN 2018002287 (ebook) | ISBN 9789352805983 (Web) | ISBN 9789352805969 (print (pb))
Subjects: LCSH: Leadership.
Classification: LCC HD57.7 (ebook) | LCC HD57.7 .J666 2018 (print) | DDC 658.4/092--dc23
LC record available at https://lccn.loc.gov/2017053031

ISBN: 978-93-528-0596-9 (PB)

SAGE Team: Manisha Mathews, Apoorva Mathur and Ritu Chopra

We dedicate this book to Dr Kobus Neethling, the founder of the 8-dimensional approach, a humble person with a brilliant mind and a beautiful heart, who has touched many people around the globe and has inspired us to integrate Whole Brain Thinking in Leadership Development.

Thank you for choosing a SAGE product!
If you have any comment, observation or feedback,
I would like to personally hear from you.

Please write to me at **contactceo@sagepub.in**

Vivek Mehra, Managing Director and CEO, SAGE India.

Bulk Sales

SAGE India offers special discounts
for purchase of books in bulk.
We also make available special imprints
and excerpts from our books on demand.

For orders and enquiries, write to us at

Marketing Department
SAGE Publications India Pvt Ltd
B1/I-1, Mohan Cooperative Industrial Area
Mathura Road, Post Bag 7
New Delhi 110044, India

E-mail us at **marketing@sagepub.in**

Get to know more about SAGE

Be invited to SAGE events, get on our mailing list.
Write today to **marketing@sagepub.in**

This book is also available as an e-book.

Brief Contents

Foreword by Kobus Neethling — xv
Preface — xvii
Acknowledgements — xxi
How to Read This Book? — xxv
Some Points to Consider — xxvii

PART 1 Welcome to the VUCA World

Chapter 1 – Challenges — 3

Chapter 2 – Face Reality — 19

PART 2 Whole Brain Thinking

Chapter 3 – Neethling Brain Instruments — 31

Chapter 4 – L1, The Rational — 52

Chapter 5 – L2, The Practical — 59

Chapter 6 – R2, The Relational — 66

Chapter 7 – R1, The Experimental — 73

Chapter 8 – Whole Brain Thinking — 81

PART 3 Lead as a Coach

Chapter 9 – A Different Mindset — 99

Chapter 10 – Integrate Coaching into Your Leadership — 112

Chapter 11 – Opening — 124

Chapter 12 – Communication — 133

Chapter 13 – Exploration	**145**
Chapter 14 – Activation	**154**
Chapter 15 – New Insights	**162**

PART 4 Transformation

Chapter 16 – Transformation	**171**
Chapter 17 – Become a Whole Brain Leader	**185**
Appendix – 360° Self-Assessment	191
References	197
About the Authors	199

Detailed Contents

Foreword By Kobus Neethling	xv
Preface	xvii
Acknowledgements	xxi
Acknowledgements from Sjoerd	xxi
Acknowledgements from Ingvar	xxiii
To All Contributors	xxiv
How to Read This Book?	xxv
Some Points to Consider	xxvii
Is This Book for Everyone?	xxvii
We Are Also Building on Other People's Material	xxvii
We Will Repeat Ourselves!	xxviii

PART 1 Welcome to the VUCA World

Chapter 1 – Challenges	**3**
Horizontal Development	3
Vertical Development	4
The VUCA Challenge	6
Leading Across Generations	7
Baby Boomers	8
Generation X	8
Generation Y	8
Generation Z	9
Levels of Development	9
Dependent	11
Independent	11
Inter-independent	11
The Achiever	12
The Individualist	12
The Strategist	13

Leadership As a Position	14
Leadership As a Process	15
The Leader As a Coach	16

Chapter 2 – Face Reality — 19

Your Challenges	21
The Value of Failure: Dig Up Your Diamonds	22
Your Journey: The Road Ahead	23
Your Toolbox Today	24
Your Fellow Travellers	25
360° Assessment	27

PART 2 Whole Brain Thinking

Chapter 3 – Neethling Brain Instruments — 31

Dr Kobus Neethling and NBI™	31
How Do You Prefer to Think?	33
How Do You Communicate?	41
How Do You Solve Problems?	43
How Do You Make Decisions?	44
How Do You Collaborate?	46
How Do You Lead?	47
The Whole Brain Approach	48
Do the Profiles!	50

Chapter 4 – L1, The Rational — 52

Thinking About 'WHAT?'	52
The Realist	53
The Analyst	54
How Does the L1, Rational, Lead?	55
How Does the L1 Leader See the World?	56

Chapter 5 – L2, The Practical — 59

Thinking About 'HOW?'	59
The Preserver	61
The Organiser	61

How Does the L2, Practical, Lead?	62
How Does the L2 Leader See the World?	63

Chapter 6 – R2, The Relational — 66
Thinking About 'WHO?'	66
The Socialiser	68
The Empathiser	68
How Does the R2, Relational, Lead?	69
How Does the R2 Leader See the World?	70

Chapter 7 – R1, The Experimental — 73
Thinking About 'WHY?'	73
The Strategist	74
The Imagineer	75
How Does the R1, Experimental, Lead?	76
How Does the R1 Leader See the World?	78

Chapter 8 – Whole Brain Thinking — 81
When You Have Your Thinking Preferences in L1, the Rational	82
When You Have Your Thinking Preferences in L2, the Practical	87
When You Have Your Thinking Preferences in R2, the Relational	88
When You Have Your Thinking Preferences in R1, the Experimental	91
How Do We All Perceive Each Other?	94
Implement Whole Brain Thinking	94
The Finishing Touch	95

PART 3 Lead as a Coach

Chapter 9 – A Different Mindset — 99
The Whole Brain Leader	100
Emotional Intelligence	101
The Ego	104

The Devil on Your Shoulder	106
Cynicism	107
Negativism	107
Unworthiness	108
Escapism	108
Procrastination	109
A Desire for Improvement	109
Chapter 10 – Integrate Coaching into Your Leadership	**112**
What Is Coaching?	113
Boss Versus Coach	115
Increase the Capacity of Others	116
From Two-way to Three-way Communication	117
Bringing Coaching into Your Workplace	118
When Is Coaching Appropriate?	119
OCEAN: Our Model for Coaching	120
O—Opening	120
C—Communication	121
E—Exploration	122
A—Activation	122
N—New insights	123
Chapter 11 – Opening	**124**
Your Presence	124
Relating to People's Potential	126
The Basics of Rapport	126
The Voice	127
Body Language	127
Trust	128
The Scale of Rapport	129
How to Build Rapport?	130
The Best Possible Outcome	131
Chapter 12 – Communication	**133**
The Power of Questions	134
Effective Questions	135

Plan Your Questions	135
How Not to Ask Questions?	136
Types of Questions	137
Principles of Listening	138
Feedback	140
Direct Communication	142

Chapter 13 – Exploration — 145
Cognitive Dissonance	146
What Is the Actual Reality?	146
Self-respect Leads to Self-confidence	147
The Gift of Reflection	149
Emotional Leverage	149
Resistance to Change	150
Ways to Explore	151

Chapter 14 – Activation — 154
Goal-setting Culture	155
The Power of Writing Things Down	155
Mistakes in Goal Setting	156
BE-SMART	157
The Whole Brain Approach	158
Verifying Your Decisions (Goals)	160
The Action Steps (5 × 5)	160

Chapter 15 – New Insights — 162
Zooming Out	163
Resisting Change	164
Self-discipline	167
Implementation and Follow-up	167

PART 4 Transformation

Chapter 16 – Transformation — 171
Connecting the Dots	172
The Need for Transformation	173

Why Should You Transform?	174
How About Your Barriers to Change?	175
What Needs To Be Transformed?	176
How to Transform?	177
Growth Opportunities	178
Who Needs Transformation?	182
What Do You Need?	182
When to Start?	183
Chapter 17 – Become a Whole Brain Leader	**185**
Grow by Sharing	185
Learn by Coaching	186
Establish Powerful and Open Networks	187
Harness the Power of Trust	188
Leveraging the Power of Generations	189
Connecting the Dots	189
Appendix – 360° Self-Assessment	191
Integrity and Ethical Management	191
Communication	192
Motivation	192
Developing Others	193
Developing Self	193
Relationship Building	194
Teamwork	194
Adaptability	195
Influencing	195
Leadership and Inspiring Others	196
Creative Thinking	196
References	197
About the Authors	199

Foreword

Many years ago, Shelby Foote wrote these beautiful words about novelty and newness: 'Of all the passions of mankind, the love of novelty most rules the mind. In every search of this, from realm to realm we roam. Our fleets come loaded with every folly home'. *The Whole Brain Leader* is new and novel.

Ingvar Jónsson and Sjoerd de Waal have made a significant contribution to both twenty-first century leadership and applied Whole Brain Thinking. The message in this book is simple: leaders who are able to put the whole brain into action can optimise organisational performance. Both Jónsson and de Waal have distinguished careers in leadership development across countries and cultures, as well as in their roles as Neethling Brain Instruments (NBI™) Whole Brain practitioners for a number of years[1]. They are ideally suited to write a leadership book from an '8-dimensional' perspective—something I believe has never been done before.

The book begins with the authors unpacking the challenges of the modern leaders and the realities they are facing (realities that keep on changing dramatically). An 8-dimensional leader is the one who not only understands his own thinking preferences but is also able to understand and respond to the thinking preferences of his team members and employees. The added value of understanding your own 8-dimensional profile is that as a leader you can surround yourself with people who complement you and assist you in areas where you lack the passion or the skills.

The authors apply a very unique approach in dissecting and examining the eight dimensions. Apart from giving an in-depth and detailed explanation of each dimension, they examine their key elements for the purpose of formulating a particular leadership

---

[1] For more information, see www.kobusneethling.co.za

style. This is a very important contribution not only to leadership design in general but also to understanding the practical value of the 8-dimensional model. It is not only a theoretical model but also one that can be applied to every facet of your personal and professional life.

The message in this book is simple: leaders who are able to put the Whole Brain into action can optimise organisational performance.

When determining success, 8-dimensional thinking moves people and companies beyond traditional measures and approaches. By using Whole Brain methodologies, your organisation and its people will be better positioned to understand, predict, position and, most likely, expand the outcomes and success of the business. Equipped with the knowledge of your own brain preferences and also those of others, you will find that the workplace can become a happy place—one where people do what they enjoy most, where they begin to understand differences and where opportunities exist for everyone to reach their full potential. The role of the leader is paramount in creating a Whole Brain culture where all of this becomes possible.

As someone who has developed more than 30 Whole Brain instruments, it is extremely heartening to see two passionate Whole Brain practitioners explore and dig deeper into the 'application possibilities' of the instruments. It is so much more meaningful and telling when an 'assessment tool' becomes alive as it does in this book. Herbert Spencer once wrote, 'The great aim of education is not knowledge, but action'. This is indeed an action book.

Kobus Neethling

The international bestselling author of more than 90 books and the developer of the NBI 8-Dimensional Instrument

Preface

> *Horizontal leadership development is about improving your skills and your way of working.*

Successful leaders know it—leadership development never stops. That was true 50 years ago, but it's even more true in the ever-changing business world we live in today.

With the introduction of the Internet in the last decades of the previous century and its explosive growth this century, we now have entered a highly interconnected era. The opportunities are endless, but so are the challenges.

Disruption is all around us. New industries and markets emerge from everywhere. Sometimes a few of them disappear as suddenly as they emerged, whereas others survive. Some make old industries and markets obsolete, resulting in the death of even large and well-established organisations. In 1998, few had heard of Google, but now, less than two decades later, it's ranked among the top five companies in terms of market value. In the previous century, Pan American World Airways and Trans World Airlines were two major airlines—icons, so to speak. Unfortunate for them, they have now vanished. Other business-disrupting airlines such as Virgin Air, Ryanair and easyJet had entered the arena.

Think of Uber, disrupting the taxi world, and Airbnb, doing the same with the hotel and bed and breakfast business. Communities of all kinds are shaking up organisations, industries, countries and even the whole world. Trying to hold on to the 'proven ways', with 'experienced leaders', has become a dangerous strategy, a nice recipe to enter the list of victims in the industry.

Organisations have to reinvent themselves in order to deal with the VUCA world, a world defined by a high level of Volatility,

Uncertainty, Complexity and Ambiguity. The acronym VUCA has been derived from the military but fits perfectly as a description of the modern business world. Given the present situation, this name also makes it easier to find solutions to deal with the problems it entails.

For leadership, this means change—a change in the way leadership should be practised. Major shifts in leadership thinking are necessary. Leadership is no longer attached to a position; it has become a process. We are moving away from the individual towards the collective approach, from 'top-down' to 'throughout the organisation', from independent to interdependent decision-making, from power in a position to power in capabilities. No matter what your organisation chart looks like, leadership is no longer for the happy few; it is something all employees have to contribute to.

The true leaders in this VUCA world accept their responsibility and work on their own development as well as on the development of their organisation. They lead as coaches, applying the power of Whole Brain Thinking. They are what we refer to as Whole Brain Leaders.

Vertical leadership development is about expanding your mindset and improving your way of thinking.

In order to reach that level, leaders have to develop vertically as well as horizontally. Horizontal leadership development is about improving your skills and your way of working. Vertical leadership development is about expanding your mindset and improving your way of thinking. Both are essential, but this book is mainly about vertical development.

We will take you on a journey. Our aim is that you arrive at the level of the Whole Brain Leader. Whole Brain Leaders inspire other leaders to join them on their journey and help their organisations to thrive in the VUCA world. They know how to adapt and create harmony from chaos.

On the vertical scale, we distinguish four levels of leadership development: the expert, the achiever, the individualist and the strategist. There are two more, less developed, levels before the expert level: the opportunist and the diplomat. However, this book has not been written for them.

The expert is the one who still depends on his original (technical) hard skills, whereas the strategist has developed his mindset in such a way that he is able to transform organisations. The development from the expert to the strategist normally takes several years. Applying the techniques presented in this book will help to speed up the process.

Following the steps, as we present them in the book, would make you aware of your reality, help you to implement Whole Brain Thinking, teach you to Lead as a Coach and get you started on the transformation necessary. Following the four steps presented in this book will not only help you deal with, but also benefit from, the VUCA world.

If your organisation depends on you, you should not hesitate; start right away, reduce the dependence and start creating a network of interdependable leaders.

Acknowledgements

This book is the result of a fruitful collaboration between two authors with a passion for leadership, thinking preferences, coaching, training and, above all, sharing.

We're both grateful for what we have experienced and learned in our (professional) lives, and have the urge to share as much as possible with you. We wish that your development will inspire those around you to deal with the VUCA world, and that our book may be a source of inspiration.

We would first like to thank Koen and Makheni Zonneveld for all their help on the Whole Brain Thinking part, and for bringing us together at the NBI™ licensee meeting in Amsterdam on 8 October 2014. We found that we had a lot in common, and it was during a Skype call in November that we decided to embark on this adventure to write a book together. The result of that decision is now in your hands.

When you write a book with someone, you really experience what synergy can accomplish. Neither of us could have created alone what we have created together. We have had intense discussions on the content of the book and the journey we wanted to organise for our readers. It has always been constructive, a classic whole brainer! The learnings have been incredible, and we are truly thankful that we grabbed this opportunity when it revealed itself.

When you write with someone, you both have your own circle of people you want to acknowledge, and some overlap will occur. Therefore, we've decided that we would write our own individual acknowledgements, as well.

Acknowledgements from Sjoerd

First of all, I would like to thank Ingvar for bringing up the idea of writing a book together. We have spent many hours working together, and that has certainly enriched my life. It was with great pleasure that I could work with Ingvar and I consider him 'The Wizard of Iceland' when it comes to design and layout. In the countless hours we have worked on the content of the book, he showed an in-depth knowledge of leadership and coaching, as well as a sharp mind and great patience.

I also wish to extend my gratitude to Sigrun, Ásbjörn and Hjördís, for their hospitality during my stays at their home in Iceland. I really felt part of their family.

Talking about family, thank you Anja for your support and patience in our own little VUCA world. You know what it's like to share your life with this restless entrepreneurial spirit and the uncertainties he causes. Thanks also to my daughter and son, Thalassa and Dexter, for their support and interest in my adventure.

I also want to thank my parents, Hanneke and Dirk. They have been my mum and dad for more than 51 years now, and celebrated their 60th wedding anniversary in 2015. Where would I have been without them?

There are still two persons left whom I want to acknowledge personally. The first is Dr Stephen Foster, who was one of my favourite professors during my MBA at Webster University. In the beginning of 2015, I had the honour of assisting him while he taught the honours class of 'Leadership' at Webster. This has definitely influenced my writing as well. I'm very grateful that he agreed to write his recommendation for this book.

The second influencer I would like to thank is Chrisoula Papadopoulou (BSc, MBA, PhD). She is a very energetic person, with incredible insights in leadership. I feel privileged to know her and am grateful that she could free up time from her busy schedule to write her recommendation.

Acknowledgements from Ingvar

Sometimes I find it hard to get my mind around all my blessings and fortune. It is with great gratitude in my heart that I thank the people who have supported me through the years and on this journey.

First, I would like to express enormous gratitude to my best friend and better half, Sigrún—your tolerance towards me and my wild ideas is admirable. I love you unconditionally.

To my four children, I say,

> Exploit every opportunity life throws at you, and never let anyone tell you what you can or cannot do. Follow your heart, and employ your head in every dream you want to turn into reality. Every journey starts with one single step. Always be kind to your fellow travellers, especially those who sometimes deserve it the least—they might actually need it the most. Most importantly, remember that you always reap what you sow.

To my parents—thank you for teaching me how to love and how to live well.

I thank my co-author, Sjoerd de Waal, for being crazy enough to write this book with me after only spending a few hours together and a couple of phone calls. I guess it takes one to know one. I also thank his wife, Anja, for her hospitality during my stay in their home in the Netherlands.

To my friends, thank you for being who you are. To the teachers from Implement (at Copenhagen Business School), thank you for helping me find my purpose in life. To my friend Kobus Neethling, thank you for your inspiration and kindness. Special thanks to Bogi Þór Siguroddsson for his time and inspiration, and last but not least, thanks to my co-workers at Profectus—our journey has only just begun!

To All Contributors

There are so many people to whom we owe a lot, and it is not possible to name them all. We've learned a lot from all the teachers in our life, and from friends and relatives. We've learned from other authors and public speakers, from people on social media and from a lot of people we've never met. All, in one way or another, have made a contribution to our life and to this book.

A huge THANK YOU to all of you!

How to Read This Book?

There are many ways to treat and read a book, and, of course, we would like you to treat books with respect. However, what you have in your hands now is an unfinished piece of art. We have included a lot of our expertise and experience, but it will never be finished. We are sure that you have your own story to tell. Add it to the book, make notes, scribble, doodle, draw and share your insights. Make it your own, but the most important thing is to actually implement what you learn on your journey. We challenge you to do the assignments and make notes of your experiences and reflect on your progress. Be proud of what you will achieve, be proud of yourself, but be even more proud of the ones you will inspire to travel with you.

Share what you will read with people around you, and challenge them to read the book as well and share their thoughts, experiences and insights. Create a learning environment, get people on the same page and let your different ways of thinking create synergy.

This book is different from the majority of leadership books. You don't have to be careful while reading it. It is designed to include your story. The value lies in what you do with it, not in its scarcity. Use it, abuse it, share it, make contributions to it and enjoy being the co-creator of the book.

As we have explained in 'Preface', we take you on a journey to become a Whole Brain Leader. In order to keep track of where you are on your journey, we have designed The Whole Brain Leader development journey. Each step on the journey corresponds with a part in our book. Before starting with a new part, we will point out where you are and connect it with where you are going.

Throughout this book, we talk about people in the male version. For us, being members of the male species, this was the most natural way to write. Of course, we also refer to our stronger counterparts, the females, when we talk about he, him or his. We encourage our female readers to take their share in Whole Brain Leadership, because you will most certainly make the greatest difference.

Enjoy your reading and learning, and don't forget to practise what you read!

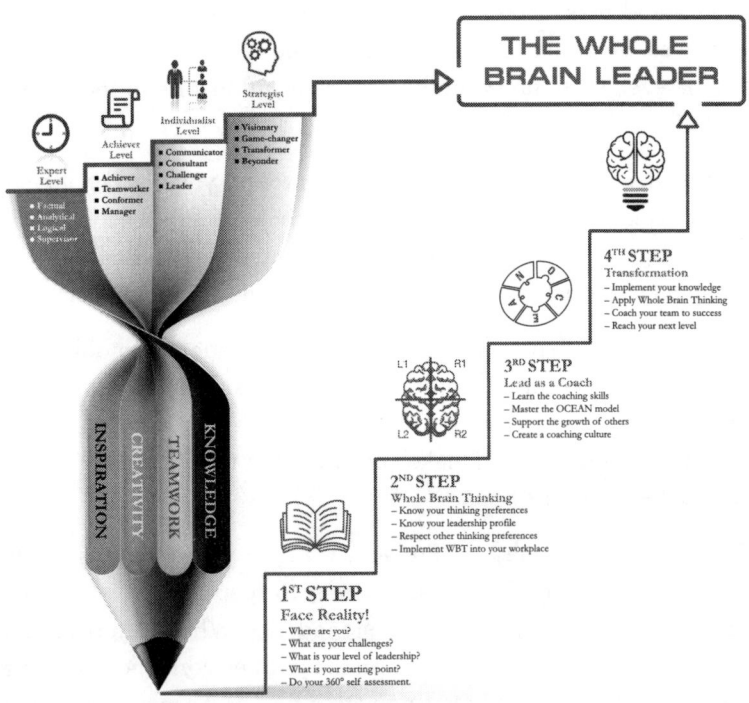

Some Points to Consider

Is This Book for Everyone?

Although we are positive that the content of our book is applicable to the majority of organisations, you may still think it's not for you.

This may very well be the case. There are indeed some markets and organisations that don't experience the influence of the VUCA world, yet. It may be too early for your organisation to go through the transformation towards leadership as a process. It can also be that your organisation is small, and individual leadership still suffices.

At the end of the book, we encourage you to roll out the transformation process to your whole organisation. In some cases, this transformation is one step too far. We feel that you should at least start applying Whole Brain Thinking yourself and start coaching as a leader. Both methods will boost your results in their own; when applied in conjunction with each other, you will experience the results to be mind-blowing. Whatever your decision may be, we will not be there to take credit nor blame for the results.

We Are Also Building on Other People's Material

Through the years, we have expanded our knowledge on leadership considerably. We have acquired a great deal of insight and knowledge from many different sources, by listening, reading, applying and so on. It's inevitable that you will discover parts of other people's wisdom throughout our book. We have done our best to refer to those we have learned from, out of respect for their intellectual rights. If, however, we have missed anything, please accept our apologies and let us know.

We Will Repeat Ourselves!

We are fully aware that in some chapters of the book you might encounter repetitions. This is intentional and a part of the learning process. Our findings through the years have taught us that repetition is much stronger than experience. So bear with us when it comes to it.

Part 1
Welcome to the VUCA World

The ultimate measure of a man is not where he stands in moments of comfort and convenience, but where he stands at times of challenge and controversy.

Martin Luther King, Jr.

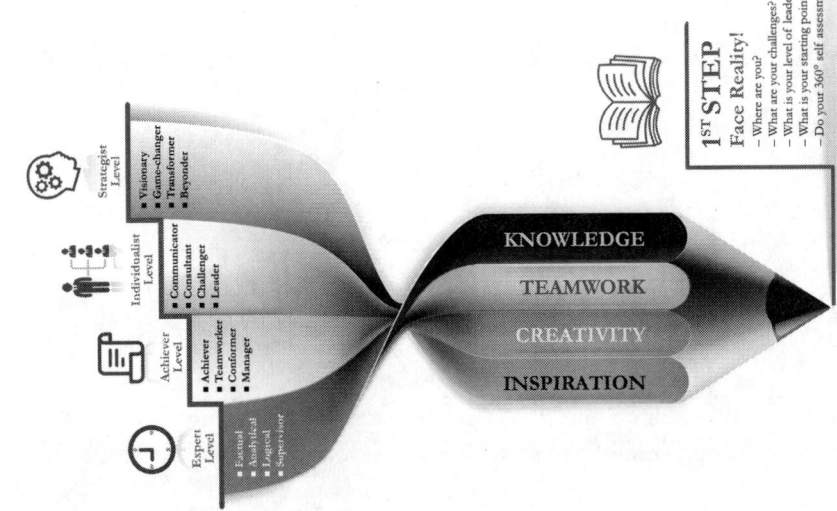

Chapter 1 – Challenges

Horizontal Development

Do you recognise this situation? You have been to a very interesting training session in which you acquired new ways of dealing with challenges in your workplace. Inspired by the newly acquired knowledge and skills, you return to work, ready to implement your new knowledge. You share with your colleagues all the hot stuff you have learnt and how that can be implemented. While telling all this to your colleagues, you experience the excitement of your aha moments again.

Are you ready to deal with the challenges ahead?

However, your colleagues don't seem as excited as you are. How come? What a disappointment! Well, they weren't there and they didn't experience the gradual build up towards the aha moment. Moreover, while you were away, they had to deal with their emergencies and are glad you're back to help them out. Before you know it, you're back in your old routine—using your old skills and knowledge to solve old and repetitive problems. You know that one day these skills and knowledge will no longer suffice. That day may arrive faster than you think.

In your career, you have learnt a lot, but somehow you feel that there's still a long way to go. However, it seems as if each training you attend only adds a little to what you already know, and implementation gets harder each time. What is the use of going to the next training? Have you reached a plateau? Is there a next level? Should you attend all those training sessions on your own, or should you bring along your colleagues as well?

Maybe you have indeed reached a plateau. Maybe just adding new skills and knowledge is no longer enough. So far, you have been working on your horizontal development, which is nothing more or less than the transfer of knowledge and skills.

Picture yourself as a container in which you pour your knowledge and skills. At a certain moment, this container is filled to the brim. Nothing substantial can be added anymore. It's time for a newer and bigger container, a newer and bigger you! Work on something else than just adding new knowledge and skills. It's time to work on the way you think, to obtain a new and improved mindset.

You're ready to go to the next level. You now have to develop yourself vertically. When you have taken the step to the next level, there is plenty room for horizontal development awaiting you again. Your container is bigger now and can be filled up again until you're ready for yet another vertical step.

Vertical Development

In the late 1980s, Dr Stephen R. Covey (1990) wrote his masterpiece *The 7 Habits of Highly Effective People*. It is the Bible for millions of leaders and it has been translated into 38 languages.

What can you do to expand your boundaries?

Why do we mention this book? Because it's about principles, and every time you read it, you find new diamonds to pick. Is that because the content changes every time you read it? No, of course not. You're developing and, therefore, other aspects in the book get your attention. You're not only developing horizontally but also vertically. Your mindset develops and, therefore, other parts of the book start to make more sense. Another very interesting read on vertical leadership development is Nick Petrie's, White Paper, *Vertical Leadership Development–Part 1, Developing Leaders for a Complex World*. It is packed with interesting research on the topic.

For a long time, it was believed that humans' mindset develops only when they grow from infant to child, from adolescent to adulthood, and that after that the brain wouldn't really develop much further. This assumption was wrong. Yes, it's more challenging than the almost automatic process from infant to adult, but people will develop their mindsets further to handle even more complex situations.

In his book, Covey (1990) describes this process as the development from dependent to independent to interdependent. The first vertical development process you accomplish by victories on yourself. The second process by victories with your environment, public victories. These developments require changes in your way of thinking; you have to adapt your mindset while growing. This is the vertical development. You grow your container, so that it can accommodate more.

Do we always need vertical leadership development? That depends on the complexity of your environment. Of course, there are still some 'non-complex' environments where independent leaders with dependent followers function very well. But increasingly so, the world becomes more interconnected and, therefore, more complex. It has become a challenge for an increasing number of leaders to succeed in such complex environments. If that is coming your way, or if you're already in the middle of it, now is probably the best time to take action.

What kinds of challenges are we talking about? Let's have a look at two of them, both real challenges in this era of never-ending change.

The VUCA Challenge

We are living in a vibrant era. We are reaching the very end of the industrial age and entering into the information age. This is changing the role of leadership considerably. Many organisations have relied (and still rely) on hierarchical organisation charts for guidance. These charts give a false impression and should be challenged! They imply that everything is under control and that the bosses should possess all knowledge.

Sadly, that is also what people expect—bosses with the overall knowledge and knowhow, able to give the 'right' orders—an era of command and control.

However, the world is changing at an unprecedented pace, which requires different ways of leadership. In the military, they have an acronym for that, VUCA.

VUCA stands for:

- **Volatility:** changes are unexpected and create an unstable environment
- **Uncertainty:** you never know what's happening next
- **Complexity:** the situation has many variables with unpredictable influences
- **Ambiguity:** many unknown factors that also might influence the situation

These factors demand a different approach to leadership. How are you dealing with VUCA? Are long-term plans still usable with changes happening all the time? How well can you predict the future with so much uncertainty? Can you still collect all the facts in order to set the right goals or is it too complex?

When the world is as ambiguous as it is nowadays, what does that mean for the accuracy of your long-term plans? Should your goals be crystal clear or just frame the big picture?

To deal with **VUCA**, you can use the same acronym:

- **Vision:** have a clear and shared vision
- **Understanding:** create a shared understanding of the context
- **Clarity:** where possible, make things simple and clear
- **Adaptability:** minimise the stiffness of the organisation. Be prepared to adapt

The challenges in the VUCA world are huge and you will learn to appreciate that they cannot be solved by just one or a few persons in the organisation. VUCA is here to stay and it requires new ways of thinking and more vertical leaders. Leaders that can adapt and tap into the collaborative powers of those they work with.

Are you such a leader or do you want to become one? Then, get ready for the next challenge!

Leading Across Generations

Different generations have different needs, abilities and thoughts. Tensions between them have always been there and are usually the result of a lack in understanding. It's up to all of us to make optimum use of all the differences instead of criticising them.

> *How many different generations populate the work floor nowadays? How do they get along?*

At this moment, there are still five generations populating the work floor. A handful of the Silent Generation (born before 1945), a decreasing amount of baby boomers (born between 1945 and 1960), Generation X (the Lost or Forgotten Generation, born between 1960 and 1980), Generation Y (the millennials, born between 1980 and 1995) and now entering the workforce is Generation Z (the Digital Teens, born between 1995 and 2002).

On the Internet, you can find loads of information on how to deal with Generation Y. Why? Well, maybe they're the ones making the transition from the industrial into the information age. At least they have a radically different approach to work than the preceding generations.

Let's take a closer look at the four major generations.

Baby Boomers

They are the biggest group, and they possess the greatest wealth of all generations. They care about health, wealth and quality. They are still very active and relatively open to new experiences.

However, it seems as if other generations have had enough of their long period of domination. They will still be around for quite a while, so maybe it's better to make use of their huge experience and insights.

Generation X

Sometimes called the Lost or Forgotten Generation. They are anti, busy and cynical. They experienced crises when they entered the market and for many of them, it was hard to find proper jobs.

In many aspects, this generation is between the baby boomers and the millennials, and can form the bridge between those two.

Generation Y

The millennials have now become the largest group in the workplace. They are often misunderstood. They have grown up with media and technology. On top of that, they know how to use it!

More than other generations, they are looking for meaning in their work. They want to make a difference and for them there's more to work than just a good salary. They are demanding and want answers now (they grew up with the Internet).

They consider professional development as one of their top priorities. The millennials have taken work-life balance a step further; they consider it an integrated part of their lives.

Millennials want enjoyable workplaces; they are tech savvy and appreciate collaboration over competition. Not a generation to be afraid of, but one to embrace!

Generation Z

This generation, also called Digital Teens, was born digital. They are used to rapid change (VUCA) even more than the millennials; however, they are easily distracted. They are more self-centred than all the other generations and live in a 'parallel universe' on social media. It is a very diverse generation with many, ever-changing, subcultures. It is hard to label them, but most probably Generation X (their parents) knows best how to work with them.

From the descriptions of the generations, you get a rough idea of their members, but please don't generalise just on the basis of the group they're in. All humans are unique and ought to be treated that way. Find the strengths in people and combine these strengths in order to lead together. Your leadership will then start to evolve from being a function into being a process.

Levels of Development

In 'Vertical Development,' we already referred to Dr Stephen Covey (1990). In his model, *The 7 Habits of Highly Effective People*, he explained the progression from dependent to independent and interdependent.

> *Is your current level of leadership sufficient to
> deal with the challenges in this day and age?*

Dependent is when you have a sense of your self-derived from connections to others. This is usually your starting point in your adolescent years or early adulthood. Dependent people often feel uncertain because of conflicting expectations from the people they value.

When you have developed into the second stage, independent, you start to reflect on your experiences in the dependent stage. From this, you gain an understanding of your own self as a self-possessed identity. Independent people don't necessarily need others to construct their self-image. For most adults, this is the highest achievable stage.

But, of course, you're not 'most adults' and you want to achieve the highest level of development possible, interdependence. In that stage, you appreciate that you can have multiple selves. Instead of 'self' being a fixed entity, it is adaptive in response to the environment.

In their article, McCauley et al. (2006) called this order of development inter-independent. This is because 'it makes the self-independent (capable of being created by the person) and dependent for its form on life's contingencies'. Interdependent is seen as being mutually dependent.

William R. Torbert has yet another way of labelling the different stages of development. He distinguishes seven 'action logics', an overall strategy that thoroughly informs individuals' reasoning and behaviour or 'the way in which they interpret their surroundings and react when their power or safety is challenged'. The first stage, the opportunist, is a stage prior to any of the other development stages and describes a rather nasty action logic, one that wants to win in any way possible.

If we combine the three stages as described by McCauley et al. (2006) with the remaining six action logics, we can produce the following overview:

Dependent

The diplomat searches for consensus and tries to avoid conflict. He helps teams to connect, but can't make difficult decisions when needed.

The expert is the person who works with facts and figures and has a logical approach. To convince an expert, you'd better have all the facts available and correct. The expert is a good individual contributor, but also expects a high level of professionalism from others. Often the expert is promoted into a management position. That's when he finds out that his emotional quotient (EQ) needs development.

Independent

The achiever is well equipped for managerial work. He meets strategic goals and knows how to juggle with his many duties. He gets things done through the team, but is not the one promoting creative thinking.

The individualist is the unconventional, not following the rules he deems unimportant. He challenges the status quo. He is unpredictable and impatient and can therefore easily irritate colleagues and bosses, especially when they are achievers. This phase can be seen as a transition phase towards the action logic strategist.

Inter-independent

The strategist is highly collaborative, challenges existing assumptions and generates transformations. We believe that the strategist is the type of leader that is needed to truly thrive in the VUCA world.

The alchemist is the highest action logic possible and it describes the leaders that make huge social transformations.

We will now explain three of the six action logics a bit deeper in order for you to determine which action logic describes you best. We also encourage you to read 'Seven Transformations of Leadership' by David Rooke and William R. Torbert (2005) to get an even better understanding of the action logics.

The Achiever

Do you think you have achieved it all?

The first level in the independent stage is the achiever. The achiever is the kind of manager who gets results. He is a team player, provides clarity around the expectations and knows how to motivate his team. Although they know how to create a positive atmosphere and work well with others, achievers are not famous for their out-of-the box thinking.

Achievers are capable of getting the team working on shared goals and resolving conflicts before they get out of hand. Many experts have trouble working with achievers. Experts use hard data and facts to convince others and they don't quite understand how the achiever can be so successful. The expert often lacks the understanding of the power collaborative networks and teams can generate. As an achiever, you understand that you have to get the experts on board as well, because they are great individual contributors.

The next step in leadership development is towards the individualist. That level is a kind of a bridge from independent to inter-independent.

The Individualist

Have you had enough of conformity?

At a certain moment, you have had enough of fitting in; you want to stand out! You start questioning what you have done as an achiever.

It no longer feels natural to you. The individualist recognises that none of the other action logics are natural either. They 'all are constructions of oneself and the world'.

The individualists communicate well with other action logics, but these logics can often annoy them too. They feel tension, and they are looking for new ways to manage and want to grow. Individualists are ready for next steps and willing to take risks to get there. If they have bosses at the achiever level, they will almost certainly clash. They run the risk of being misunderstood, because they tend to think (far) out of the box.

The individualist doesn't look at goals as given facts, but wants to find out how much they are worth. He will actively search for better, and more meaningful goals to achieve, goals that will have the highest impact on the organisation. For many leaders, becoming an achiever is the highest level possible. High potentials will proceed to the individualist level. With the right attitude and professional coaching, they can even become strategists.

The Strategist

Are you ready for transformational thinking?

Strategists are rare. Less than 5% of the leaders reach this level. The strategist is a visionary and is able to transform people and whole organisations. Strategists see organisational change as an iterative process. They know that people usually resist change and feel comfortable dealing with that. They are very effective in change processes and can adapt plans to newfound realities. Where the individualist challenges goals to discover the ones that will have the highest impact on the organisation, the strategist takes it even beyond the organisation. The strategist also considers the impact on society.

Strategists communicate effectively with all other levels and create shared visions that encourage both personal and organisational transformations. Strategists are fascinated with personal and organisational relationships and keep a sharp eye on national and international developments. They are socially conscious and highly collaborative, within as well as outside the organisational boundaries. Ethics are key!

We consider the strategist to be the kind of leader who thrives best in the VUCA world, and it is our goal to get you to that level and take it even further. The strategist is the one we need in order to realise transformations in leadership thinking. It doesn't need to be lonely at the top!

Leadership As a Position

How much longer will we continue to use the hierarchical organisation charts?

Organisation charts usually give clarity about who is working where and how the hierarchical relations are defined. They give an overview of who the leaders are and who should follow. Communication goes top-down and bottom-up as well as from left to right. Everyone should follow the hierarchical structure!

If you still believe in this kind of structures, we have bad news for you. The old mechanistic industrial approach has indeed functioned for quite a long while now, but the world is changing and it is changing fast! Where people were seen as cogs in a machine, we now see a more organic approach, where networks emerge and expand and boundaries disappear. People should no longer be placed in boxes.

Information and knowledge is everywhere. It doesn't reside with just the formal leaders. In organic systems, you see a much higher capability of adapting to the environment.

Leadership as a position is also becoming less effective when dealing with the challenges. People cannot expect a leader to have all the answers, and the leader shouldn't pretend he does.

The most successful organisations nowadays behave like living networks, with connections being made and broken all the time. Communication cannot be managed as assumed in organisational charts or quality handbooks. Prepare yourself for the VUCA world and approach leadership as a process instead of as a position.

Leadership As a Process

What have you discovered about (your) leadership so far: not only in this chapter but also in your career? Have you experienced the power of true collaboration? Have you worked, or are you working, in a transparent organisation?

Who else can contribute to the leadership process?

Many older, established, organisations still cling to the old age and will experience challenges transforming into more adaptive systems. It takes courage of individualists or, better yet, leadership on higher levels to make those transformations happen.

Younger, emerging, organisations have already adapted their leadership to their environments. This transformation is never a guarantee for survival, but it is one of the most important steps in the right direction.

In order to thrive in a VUCA environment, you should seriously consider to tap into the collective and collaborative powers of the organisation. This book gives you an opportunity to take you and your team on a journey. Together you can determine a higher meaning for your team. What are the shared vision, mission and values you adopt? Not something one person dictates, but clear and simple statements developed by you and your team.

What are the long- and short-term goals? Again, decided upon by the assembled team. Use the expertise from the front-liners as well. Have creative thinking processes in place to reflect on the directions the team takes (and has taken) and improve where possible. Involvement will foster engagement, and more people will actively search for further improvements.

The Leader As a Coach

If done correctly, coaching is always a win-win activity. Both the coach and the coachee will gain new and important insights. What kind of a leader are you? Do you coach the ones you lead? If yes, how?

> *Who learns the most from coaching:
> the coach or the coachee?*

If you have recognised yourself as an achiever, individualist or strategist, then, without doubt, you have already done your share of coaching. If you're working at the expert level, you will have some catching up to do, and most certainly you need some coaching yourself.

Why is it important to coach the ones you lead? As a leader, it is one of your primary tasks, and within your area of responsibility, to develop others and to bring out the very best in them. Especially now that leadership is moving away from being a function towards being a process, it becomes a high priority for all involved to display true and authentic leadership. As a formal leader, you are the one to take the lead, without having second thoughts about your position. For the sake of your own development, it will become essential for you to appreciate and welcome the changes that will emerge from leadership as a process.

What do you think? Can your organisation rely on just a few formal leaders or should you pull more people out of their comfort zones in order to implement leadership in every position?

How sustainable is the knowledge of the few compared to the knowledge of all? Will it be sufficient in the long run? If you, after reading this, are left with a feeling of losing power and authority, you probably still operate at the dependent level, as an expert or below. The good news is that your learning curve will be extremely steep through the rest of the book. Give in—don't give up!

The world around you keeps changing and you will benefit greatly by taking an adaptive approach to those changes. That means, start coaching your team and invite them on board of the leadership!

How to get them on board? Coach, share and challenge! Be as transparent as possible, involve them in your decision-making processes and challenge them to leave their comfort zones regularly. Ask for their advice, even if you have already figured out the solutions. Listen and be quiet as they speak. Listen to understand, not to react. Share your insights after they have done their talking. Ask questions, challenge their insights in a positive way and jointly reach superior solutions.

- Who should be on the coaching list? Everyone!
- Should you do all the coaching yourself? No!

When you develop an organisation of leaders and build on trust and transparency, everyone can, and should, become a coach. Create a coaching culture and watch the energy and engagement rise, once you've brought coaching into the workplace. Look what happens to the bureaucracy and the speed and quality of decision-making. Later in this book, we will dedicate several chapters to the leader becoming a coach.

It's that important!

- What do you need to become the change agent that will help your organisation to be equipped to deal with the challenges of the information age?
- In what ways is VUCA challenging your organisation?
- How can you create an adaptive environment?
- Who are the leaders within your organisation?
- How do you get them on board of your leadership?

Chapter 2 - Face Reality

Your starting point.

> *How do you experience the world around you?*
> *What role do you play in your organisation?*

In the previous chapter, we have discussed the challenges organisations and their leaders are facing. We have also looked at several levels of vertical development and indicated the levels of development needed to transform people and organisations.

Development from one level to the next often happens when you run into your limitations. With every level, a whole new world is opening up for you, with new opportunities for further development.

One such transition is from the expert to the achiever, where you find that it is not all about the facts, but also that EQ plays a major role as well.

In order to know how you have to develop yourself, it's important to understand at which level you are now. The fact that you are reading this book indicates that either you're at the very end of the dependent level or, more probably, have just entered into independency. If you are still at the expert level, this book will be a real challenge for you to comprehend, and some of the issues will not resonate immediately. For the expert, the title of this book, *The Whole Brain Leader*, may sound too soft. He still relies mostly on his hard skills. Nonetheless, continue reading, expand your comfort zone, jump on the bandwagon and enjoy the ride. Another idea could be to find an achiever within your organisation to travel with you on this journey. It may add to the experience and help you in comprehending the higher levels of thinking.

It's very important for you to face reality at this point. If your ego is whispering something like 'Why am I listening to this? I know what I'm doing', then it's a clear sign that you most probably need this book to reach your next level.

If you have already made the transition to the achiever level, this book is definitely for you.

We do think that you are either on the achiever or at the individualist level. Why? Because you have found that there is more to leadership. You know the power of emotional intelligence and you want to expand your learning. As an achiever, you've probably set goals for your own development and appreciate that you're still on a development journey.

The further you are in your development, the more you will challenge the goals given. You know that there is more. You will discover and redefine many things that you have taken for granted until now. You don't feel happy with the restrictions laid upon you and start doubting the efficacy of the organisational structure. You begin to understand that there are other possibilities of the structure, less artificial and with a higher adaptability. These are all signs that you have entered the individualist level.

You will also discover that more colleagues have difficulties understanding your drive, but it doesn't get under your skin. For you it's important to realise that they haven't developed as far as you have. Don't let it fuel your ego; it doesn't make you more important. They just haven't got your insights—yet. Your task is to help them develop and grow. Hence, the emphasis we will put on the coaching tasks the leader has.

Allow us to give you the tools to provoke your thinking in order to develop yourself to the strategist level. You won't get there immediately, but you will be ready to start and eventually complete the journey.

Which of the levels resonates most with you? Be completely honest to yourself and reflect on situations at work, where you can find hints. How do you react in stressful situations? How do you feel when you're in these situations and how do you feel afterwards? Did you reach out for help? Who helped you and with what? Defining your starting point, your present level, is vital to start your journey.

Your Challenges

In the previous chapter, we gave some suggestions to deal with VUCA. Unfortunately, it will not be easy. You might need to go through a change process or, maybe better, accept continuous change and adaptability as the new norm. Can you control that process and develop clear goals that have to be met? Or should the process be more reflected by the big picture, an underlined purpose?

Do you recognise areas for growth?

The strategist realises that purpose defines the goals. Purpose is the core; goals should be adapted to the situation, not the other way around. Goals should be driven by their purpose, not by individual, or short-term benefits.

How will you define your purpose? Who do you need to involve? What will be the outcome? There are more questions than answers. In order to deal with VUCA, you need input from all the players, from the frontline workers, the organisers, the customers—in short, from as many stakeholders as possible. You need to keep asking questions and feed the answers back into the organisation. Adapt your plans where necessary and keep things as simple as possible.

You can learn to look at situations from different perspectives in order to get a bigger picture. Acknowledge that different people have different thinking preferences. Appreciate the power and introduce Whole Brain Thinking into your organisation. You have people challenging the status quo and people who want to preserve stability. There is, however, an outside world that is constantly changing. In order to deal with that, you need people who ask **why** as well as people who ask **what**, **how** and **who**. When you can harmonise these different thinking preferences, you can better orchestrate the way you handle VUCA.

As a leader, you can benefit enormously by learning the methods of coaching and passing that knowledge on. By coaching each other and using the strengths of Whole Brain Thinking, you can create an adaptive organisation.

In the next part of this book (Chapters 3–8), we will explain the thinking preferences and Whole Brain Thinking. In Part 3 (Chapters 9–15), we will help you to set up your coaching and develop your coaching skills.

The Value of Failure: Dig Up Your Diamonds

What is failure? Is it bad or can it also be good?

Failure is feedback, nothing more and nothing less. Most leaders and organisations understand that you can learn from your failures, but most fail to act accordingly. Too often, they play the blame game, causing co-workers to sweep problems under the carpet.

These are dangerous habits. You need to have as much clarity as possible in order to make the best decisions possible. Therefore, be careful how you react when someone reports a failure. Embrace the fact that he had the courage to be a messenger of bad news.

That brings us to the next points: not all failures are bad and many are inevitable.

Only a small percentage is blameworthy. There's also a large range of reasons for failures to happen. On one end of the spectrum, you find the person that chose to violate a procedure or regulation, and on the other end, the labs that deliberately fail, having learned to embrace failure in order to come to the right solutions as quickly as possible. This latter kind of failure is definitely good and people working in those environments value failure for what it brings.

In business, you often have to deal with incomplete information, uncertain circumstances and complex processes. Sometimes big failures are inevitable because of that, but more often they are the result of a string of small failures. It is key to discover these small build-ups. Understand why they happen, how you can prevent them and how you can learn from them. You don't learn as much from the games you win!

Have a look at yourself and your career so far. Which failures have you experienced? What did that do to you? Have you brought them up or did you swipe them under the carpet? Did you pick up the diamonds from those failures? If not, reflect on your failures and look if you can spot them now. They are sparkles in your development.

When people are in the middle of a mess, it occupies all their attention. At that moment, they seldom realise that the biggest failures usually also lead to the biggest leaps in their development. A good coach would ask: 'What did you learn?' Remember, even when you fall flat on your face, you still move forward.

Your Journey: The Road Ahead

Place yourself on a ship. What do you see when you look backwards? And what do you see when you look ahead? Of course, the ship is a metaphor for your life. When you look back, you'll see the wash of the ship, the course it has sailed and the course your life took so far. You are what and where you are because of the decisions you have taken so far. Your ego might be a bit offended now because it loves to play the 'blame game', but sometimes it's best to accept the reality, the nature of cause and effect.

When you walk to the front of the ship, the bow, what do you see? There is no wash. You still have the opportunity to set your course. What will be your true north? Where do you want to travel to?

When you look further over the edge, where the ship ploughs through the surface, you will see white water. The rougher the sea and the faster you sail, the more white water you will see. Compare that with your situation. Are you in the fast lane? Is your ship seaworthy? Can it withstand storms? How far can you see? Where is your horizon?

Imagine that you're at the achiever's level, and you want to become a strategist. What does that mean for you? How do you prepare your journey? Will it be a fast journey or will it take longer? Is it a smooth sail, or do you have to endure rough seas, going through uncharted territory? How do you avoid running aground? What do you expect to see while travelling? What will you learn?

Developing from an achiever to a strategist will usually take some years. Years of perseverance and regular reflections. We advise you to use this book as your road map, travel guide and diary. We urge you to take notes on your journey. Read them regularly and reflect on what you have learned. That is a strong statement to yourself, you're taking your personal development seriously.

Expanding your mind is entering into an unknown territory. Prepare your journey. Take your time reading, think things over and paint a mental picture of your expectations. How will you handle barriers and obstacles? Can you think of any alternatives? What will you learn when you have failures or setbacks? Remind yourself why you are on this journey. Why is it important for you? The bigger the **WHY**, the bigger the chance you will succeed!

Your Toolbox Today

What is in your toolbox now and which other tools do you need?

Let's assume that you have developed from an expert to an achiever, from being dependent to independent, and that you have a well-filled toolbox. Now you want a bigger box to add new tools you are going to collect on your journey.

You already have the skills to collaborate, you know how to prioritise and plan. You challenge and support your team, and you have great communication skills and considerable knowledge of management issues. You have created your networks and know where to find crucial information. You operate well within your organisation.

So far, you have conformed to the expectations laid upon you, but challenging them was one bridge too far. You want to take your next step. You have discovered that beyond your present goals and plans, there is a different world—a world in which the individualists and strategists challenge the goals you're working on now, a world that cries out for creative thinkers, a VUCA world that needs leaders who know that both the industrial age and top-down management are relics from the past. They have the knowledge, vision and ability to transform organisations accordingly.

Leaders within that world find new ways of collaboration. They work in networks that adapt their size and structure. It takes a higher level of thinking, comprehension and action. It also takes courage to aim for that higher level and to work towards it. Leaders in this league get out of their comfort zones and take risks. The predictability of success is not what you are used to. But let's be frank! At this moment, you're probably overestimating this.

In the coming chapters, you will work on achieving that mindset. In other words, you are going to work on your vertical leadership development.

Your Fellow Travellers

When a leader crosses the line from being dependent to independent, he starts to realise the power of synergy. His personal development is no longer just about his development. He knows that he has to put more emphasis on his fellow travellers. They will start at a different level, and it's the leader's responsibility to develop them to their next level as well. Their mindsets need to grow to be able to handle more complex situations.

In order to make your journey interesting and challenging for them as well, you should develop a deep understanding of their thinking preferences. For that, we will introduce Neethling Brain Instruments (NBI™) in the next chapters. We will explain how you can create synergy by bringing different thinking preferences together, that is, harness the Whole Brain Thinking approach. When you experience that power, you will also be able to coach your fellow travellers more effectively.

In order to further increase the diversity of the group, we also challenge you to get members from different generations on board. Give them the opportunity to coach each other and share each other's points of view. Baby boomers can be great mentors for Generation Y, and Generation Y members can teach the baby boomers a lesson as well. Generation X are often well equipped to help Generation Y with their first steps in management. Generation Y is sometimes the best to ask challenging questions about Generation X's working methods. The key is always openness and the willingness to learn from each other.

When you elevate your companions to higher levels, they too will be better equipped to deal with VUCA, giving them more confidence to take better decisions and choose the right actions.

Most likely, you have visited many of the places that are still new for your companions. It will become your role to be their mentor. Be patient. You may have 'been there—done that', but they certainly haven't. If you look through their eyes, you may even discover new things yourself. Again an opportunity to reflect and learn. Use your experience when you travel, but be open to all the new experiences as well. Above all, enjoy the journey!

360° Assessment

You know yourself best, don't you?

When you are preparing for your journey, it's good to have a reality check before you leave. Assess yourself now and let others assess you too. We have put together a questionnaire; you can find it in the Appendix and use it to assess yourself. At given intervals, you may want to do it again to track your progress.

It is a 360° assessment, which means that you will get a more complete picture of yourself when you also ask your subordinates, peers and bosses to fill in the questionnaire. Be aware, this is the last time we will talk in this hierarchical manner. We want to show you that there are alternatives for this Newtonian thinking.

In the 360° assessment, you could benefit from including the views of different generations and people with different thinking preferences. You should expect to receive some unfavourable comments. Especially when you've created an environment where people are able to trust each other, the feedback you'll receive will be meant to make you better in your leadership.

From the feedback you receive, you can make personal development plans. Ask for clarification where necessary, but don't go into denial. Change starts with acceptance, and let's be fair; you probably have some blind spots to work on. We all have. You can also download the questionnaire from www.wholebrainleader.com

- How can you create a plan to grow to your next level of leadership?
- How will that next level positively impact your leadership?
- Who will benefit from your development?
- How will they benefit from your development?
- Which challenges that you are facing now will be solved when you reach your next level?

Part 2
Whole Brain Thinking

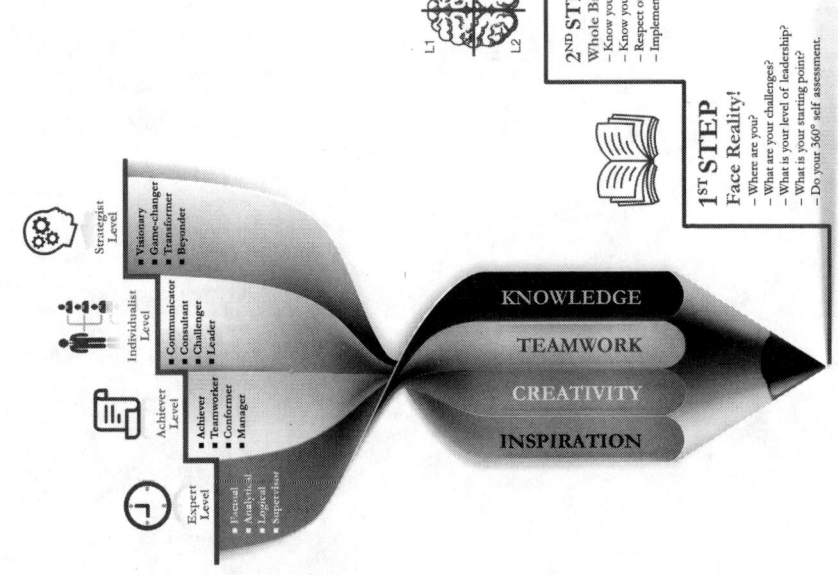

Chapter 3 – Neethling Brain Instruments

In this chapter, we introduce Neethling Brain Instruments (NBI™). It's the first chapter of six in this part that we contribute to Whole Brain Thinking.

In order to become a Whole Brain Leader, it's essential that you gain a thorough understanding of the different thinking preferences. In this chapter, we explain how these thinking preferences can improve your communication, problem-solving, decision-making, collaboration, and leadership in general. In Chapters 4–8, we will elaborate further on each quadrant and their dimensions.

Dr Kobus Neethling and NBI™

Dr Kobus Neethling holds six degrees, including two masters, a doctorate and a post-doctorate. He has written more than 90 books and 9 TV series, including a number of international bestsellers: *Creativity Uncovered*, *Very Smart Parents* and version two of *Am I Clever or Am I Stupid* (which has sold more than 200,000 copies).

One of the most amazing parts of our body is our brain. It's, therefore, not hard to understand that, through the ages, many scientists have researched this specific part. President Obama said in one of his speeches, 'We know less about the brain than we know about the moon'. The brain greatly determines the quality of our lives. It's literally the headquarters of our body, the nerve centre that determines what happens in the rest of the body.

It decides which information we take in and how it is processed and acted upon. It's quick and can perform many tasks simultaneously. Most tasks we take for granted. It can't hurt to become more aware of what is going on in the brain, and NBI™ is, in our opinion, one of the very best tools to frame that understanding. By understanding our ways of thinking, we can communicate better, collaborate easier, solve problems faster and make better decisions by including others with different thinking preferences.

It is believed that Hippocrates was the first physician who attributed thoughts, ideas and feelings to the brain. In those times, the majority believed that thinking came from the heart. He also discovered that the brain was divided into two halves and that each half had its own specific functions. He came to that conclusion because soldiers that suffered injuries on the left side of the head, also had difficulties with their speech, whereas soldiers with injuries on the right side of the head didn't have these problems.

In our previous century, there has been more research conducted on the functions of both halves. In 1981, Roger Sperry received the Nobel Prize for his split-brain theory and research. It became apparent that the two brain halves control the opposite body halves and also completely different aspects of thought and action.

Dr Kobus Neethling was part of a team that researched brain dominance, and they discovered that the way we think could be categorised. Extensive international research since 1980 resulted in the development of NBI™. Dr Kobus Neethling first developed the four-quadrant NBI™ for adults, and from this, he and his team used similar methodologies to develop other brain instruments (e.g., the leadership skills, sports and job instrument).

In 2004, after further extensive research, Dr Neethling developed the 8-dimensional profile that divides each quadrant into two dimensions, giving an even more precise insight into the thinking preferences.

Since the brain is subject to an enormous amount of neuroscientific research, many new discoveries have been made in the meantime. One of the discoveries is that certain ways of thinking, logical or creative, are not necessarily located at the left or right side of the brain. With modern technology, it has been found that specific thinking processes are related to specific areas in the brain. For logical thinking, for example, also areas at the physical right side of the brain will be activated. In brain scans, you will see specific clusters lighting up for specific thinking.

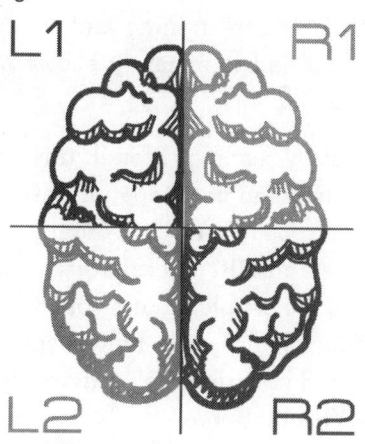

In order not to make things unnecessarily complicated, with the NBI™ profiles, we continue using the metaphor of the left and right sides of the brain, with L1, L2, R1 and R2 as the names for the four quadrants. L1 and L2 are the quadrants that refer to the metaphorical left side of the brain and R1 and R2 to the metaphorical right side of the brain.

All four quadrants have been subdivided into two dimensions. These eight dimensions have all been added to their specific quadrant. Again, this is a visual representation, but the real brain activities related to these dimensions may very well take place in other areas of the brain.

How Do You Prefer to Think?

Have you ever thought about why other people see things differently?

Understanding your thinking preferences, and the thinking preferences of the people around you, can open your gates to greatness. NBI™ is the perfect framework to understand our different thinking preferences and the significant impact those differences have on almost every aspect of the organisation. It offers you the insight and understanding of human behaviour that can help you and your organisation reach the next level of development.

Thousands of organisations, schools, consultants and coaches around the world are currently working with the NBI™. There are other instruments offering similar solutions, but we prefer the NBI™ in our training and coaching because it is easy to understand and it instantly shows how and where you can develop yourself.

Just by reading through this part of the book, you will not only understand but, hopefully, also start to embrace the diverseness of the people in your organisation. Although you may not have taken an NBI™ profile (yet), you will start to recognise yourself and the people around you in the different quadrants of the brain. You will also learn how to spot the clues in others and your surroundings, thus helping you to adjust your leadership style to each situation.

With NBI™, we define four quadrants, L1, L2, R1 and R2, being left top, left bottom, right top and right bottom, respectively. Remember, these quadrants have their activities spread all over the brain, but we use left and right as well as top and bottom metaphorically.

NBI-8-dimensional brain profile. R2 dominant supported by R1.

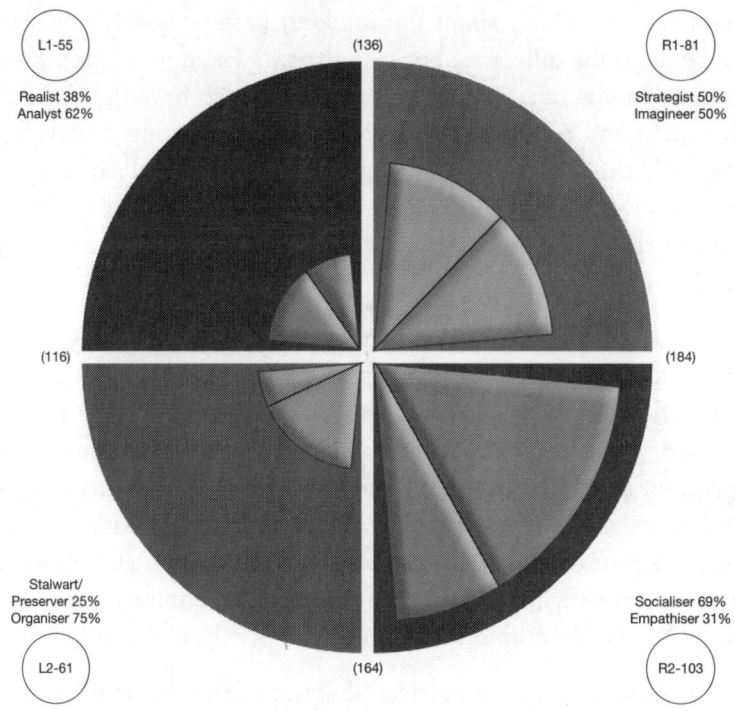

Typically, an NBI™ thinking preference profile shows one or two dominant preferences and one or two supporting preferences. The profile shows a score for each quadrant and the four scores together always add up to 300. The scores are divided in five categories, ranging from 'very low preference' to 'very high preference'. The 'high' and 'very high' scores determine your dominant preference(s).

In the picture above, you see a typical example of a profile with dominant thinking preferences in R2, supported by R1. When using and interpreting NBI™, it's important to understand that there are no best or worst thinking preferences. There are instruments that measure skills and other instruments that measure preferences.

Here we are talking about the thinking preferences. It's vital to understand the difference between the two. Having thinking preferences in one quadrant doesn't mean you also have the skills in that quadrant. You may never have had the opportunity to develop them. On the other hand, you may have developed skills in a quadrant you don't prefer to think in. These differences may, however, cause stress and dissatisfaction at work, both in the short and long terms.

Knowing your thinking preferences could help you understand which kind of work suits you best. As Steve Jobs said, 'The only way to do great work is to love what you do'. With your NBI™ profile at hand, you can now choose to do what you love (in your dominant quadrant or quadrants), and better yet, distribute responsibilities and tasks more effectively by considering the thinking preferences of your team. Let's have a look at the characteristics of each quadrant and its dimensions. See if you can recognise yourself (or others) in the descriptions.

For all dimensions, we emphasise that not *all* the characteristics of that dimension will resonate with the person having his thinking preferences in that dimension. However, most of them will. You can go to extremes and make a caricature of all the dimensions, and for the purpose of learning and enjoying the journey, we will do that in the following chapters.

An L1 thinker wants to see real facts and figures. He is a logical thinker and doesn't display too much emotion. He is living in the present tense and is focused on the bottom line. He likes things to be done his way. After all, he is basing his decisions on facts, so how can he be wrong? 'It's my way or the highway' could be his favourite saying.

Within the L1 quadrant, we have two dimensions: the *realist* and the *analyst*. There are, of course, similarities in their thinking but also quite some differences.

The realist can be described as someone who:

- Prefers clear and concise information
- Weighs the pros and cons of ideas and plans
- Doesn't want to be distracted
- Focuses on a specific goal or outcome
- Wants to understand all possible consequences
- Wants to make quick and clear decisions

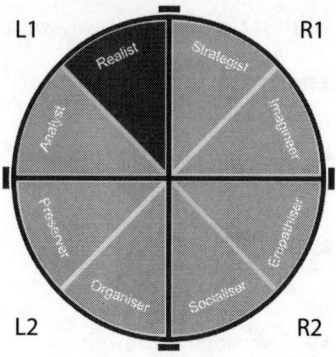

The analyst can be described as someone who:

- Wants to get to the core of things
- Wants to be involved in financial matters
- Sets priorities
- Calculates and examines
- Monitors performance
- Prefers certainty

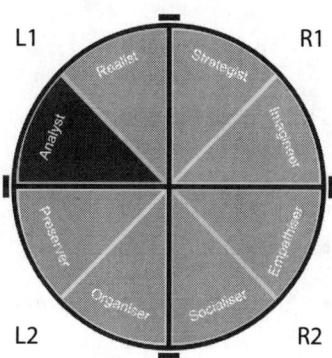

An L2 thinker is task and result driven. He prefers stability and is risk avoidant. An L2 thinker thinks in rules and regulations, loves to make plans and knows how to get things done. He prefers experienced hands-on people and works in a sequential and structured way. He is detail oriented. 'The devil is in the details' could be a quote from an L2 thinker.

Within the L2 quadrant, we have the *preserver* and the *organiser*.

The preserver can be described as someone who:

- Prefers the traditional and well-proven approach
- Points out that there are rules and regulations to be obeyed
- Appreciates/demands punctuality
- Prefers experienced people
- Works in a methodical and safe manner
- Values loyalty

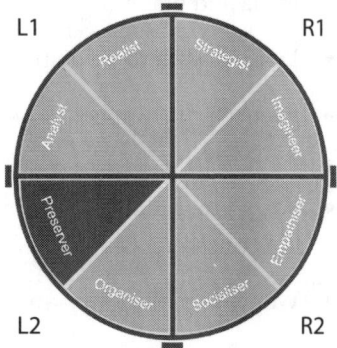

The organiser is a person who:

- Has a hands-on mentality
- Gets things done
- Gets ideas implemented and kicked into action
- Works according to schedule
- Has extensive to-do lists
- Organises tasks and supervises progress

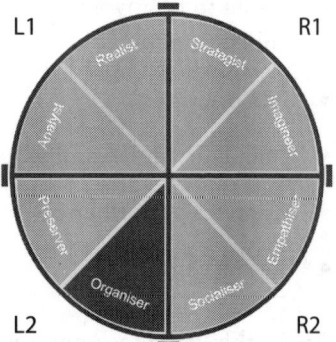

The R2 person loves to work with people, either in 'one-on-one' or 'one-to-many' situations. They love to communicate and will take care that R1, L1 and L2 thinkers get supported. However, the ideas, facts and plans have to be in line with their value systems. The R2 person is highly participative and focuses more on people than on the rational processes. You may hear a person with an R2 preference saying, 'It's nice to be important, but it's more important to be nice!'

The R2 quadrant can be subdivided into the *socialiser* and the *empathiser*.

The socialiser is a person who:

- Likes to work in groups
- Brings people together
- Shares information
- Is energetic in the company of others
- Inspires the group
- Prefers to reach consensus

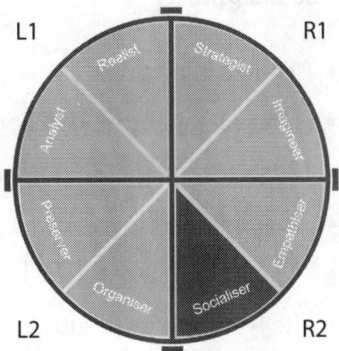

The empathiser is a person who:

- Assists and reaches out
- Serves others through a caring and sensitive attitude
- Depends on intuition
- Places needs of others above his own
- Encourages others to achieve

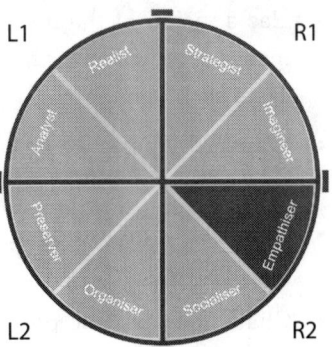

The R1 thinker is the risk taker who challenges the status quo. He is an idea hamster. The R1 embraces the big picture, but easily loses interest when the attention shifts towards details and statistics. R1 asks 'why' or rather 'why not?'

'When nothing is sure, everything is possible' describes an R1 perfectly.

The R1 quadrant is subdivided in the *imagineer* and *strategist* dimensions.

The imagineer:

- Thinks in pictures
- Uses metaphors and images
- Flirts with 'impossible' ideas
- Is a dreamer
- Thinks far out of the box
- Reflects and meditates

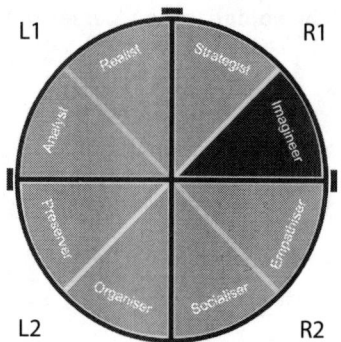

The strategist:

- Connects the past to the future
- Has a vision of the future and makes predictions and forecasts based on that
- Wants to experience new endeavours
- Considers a multitude of possibilities
- Challenges existing procedures
- Is not risk aversive

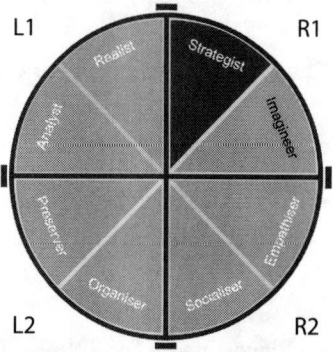

Be aware that everyone has a combination of dimensions they prefer to think in. Also, keep in mind that nobody 'owns' a whole dimension. Not all aspects will resonate with you in the same magnitude, and some aspects from other—less preferred—dimensions may indeed appeal to you as well. The deeper understanding you gain of your own thinking preferences, the easier it will be for you to determine those of others and to collaborate with them more effectively.

How Do You Communicate?

The essence of communication is to convey a message that is understood the way it was meant. How do you convey such a message?

In a communication process, you have an encoding and decoding step. In order to convey your message in the most effective and clear manner, you can best encode your message in a language that is understood by the receiver. In the whole brain communication, this would be the language of the dominant quadrant or dimension of the receiver. That is easy when you're only communicating with one person, but when you communicate to a whole group, you have to take all quadrants into account. Therefore, it is good to know the core questions for each quadrant:

L1 asks WHAT?

L2 asks HOW?

R2 asks WHO?

R1 asks WHY?

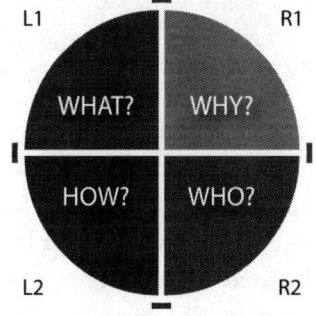

Knowing this, we can now dive in a bit deeper into each quadrant.

L1 wants the communication to be accurate. Come up with real facts. It must be coherent, realistic and clear. The communication should be focused and without any unnecessary clutter. Bringing in research, calculations and/or statistics increases the chances of being heard, understood and accepted by the L1 thinker.

L2 wants to know everything about the 'how'. Be well prepared, organised and don't skip important details. When you talk about plans and schedules, you will have the attention of the L2 thinker. Be cautious and correct, but above all, punctual. The L2 thinker gladly helps you to discover the flaws in your plans. So if you don't like criticism on your brilliant ideas, don't talk to the L2. On the other hand, if you want to improve your plans, implement them and turn them into reality, L2 is the one to talk to.

R2 is caring, so your communication should involve people and you must show that you are truly concerned about them as well. R2 people like to listen and communicate. They like to share information and are able to encourage and inspire others to engage in the endeavours as generated by R1, validated by L1 and planned by L2 people. For R2 thinkers, connections are important.

The R1 thinker likes to be surprised. He wants to embark on new endeavours; he is a pioneer, looking for new frontiers. If you want to engage the R1, leave out the details and paint the big picture. This person needs very little encouragement to produce numerous ideas. If you are looking for fresh new ideas to spice up your business, try to engage an R1 person in the process. Synthesise, fantasise and imagine. Everything is possible!

Throughout the book, we will talk about the **L1, L2, R1 or R2** and add something like **person, people or thinker** to it. When we do so, we mean people with **L1-, L2-, R1- or R2 thinking preferences**. People are **not defined by their thinking preferences, but they have** these thinking preferences. Please be aware of this subtle distinction! The same is valid for the eight dimensions.

How Do You Solve Problems?

Each quadrant has its own preferred way to solve problems. What is yours?

Problem-solving is a key activity for many people, either solving their own problems or those of others. Big or small, complex or simple, problems are part of our lives. Many organisations (if not all) are built around solving problems of others. It's a business.

It's also a process with some basic steps. None of the thinking preferences are equally strong in each step, so—again—use the whole brain.

The basic steps for problem-solving are:

1. Define the problem
2. Generate alternatives
3. Evaluate alternatives
4. Implement solutions

For each step, there are substeps and special techniques which we will not explain in-depth. We will look into the characteristics of each quadrant when it comes to problem-solving and which quadrants will feel comfortable with each step.

L1	R1
- Analyses the facts at hand - Gathers all relevant information - Takes a neutral stance and avoids emotions	- Is an intuitive problem solver - Considers the big picture - Visualises

(Continued)

L1	R1
- Looks at the problem-solving process in a rational way - Focuses on accuracy	- Generates ideas by the dozens - Dares to take risks - Stimulates idea generation with others - Is future oriented
L2	**R2**
- Arranges the facts in categories - Thinks sequentially (step by step) - Checks if the facts are valid - Is critical towards (new) ideas - Looks into the details - Thinks practically and prefers proven methods	- Considers the consequences for the people involved - Is concerned with values and ethics - Is eager to share ideas - Collaborates - Brings human insights to ideas - Is emotionally engaged

How Do You Make Decisions?

How many decisions have you made today?
Were they the right ones?

We make hundreds of decisions every day—some consciously, but most unconsciously. All those decisions determine the quality of our lives. In business, making the right decisions is crucial. It determines if an organisation thrives, survives or dies.

With such high-impact consequences, it's essential that you apply Whole Brain Thinking in all important decision-making processes. Every team member needs to understand his own thinking preferences and those of the team.

In the Whole Brain decision-making process, we need the best from every quadrant!

We need L1 thinking:	We need R1 thinking:
<ul><li>to determine the real problem, based on the analysis of the situation</li><li>when technical and statistical insights are needed</li><li>when critical thinking is needed to select the best logical alternatives</li><li>when the decision involves financial consequences</li><li>when we want to respect the profit part of the 'triple bottom line'</li></ul>	<ul><li>to look at the big picture</li><li>to come up with alternatives</li><li>when we need innovative ways to implement the decision</li><li>when the decision results in change processes</li><li>to connect the past to the future</li></ul>
We need L2 thinking:	**We need R2 thinking:**
<ul><li>to consider the organisational aspects of a plan</li><li>to execute the plan</li><li>to fault-find ideas and plans</li><li>to assess if the decision is practical</li><li>when we have to schedule the plans</li></ul>	<ul><li>when interpersonal aspects play an important role</li><li>when the decision has to be communicated effectively</li><li>when ethical matters have to be assessed</li><li>for critical thinking about the best decision for the people involved</li><li>when we want to respect the people and planet parts of the 'triple bottom line'</li></ul>

The decision-making process is closely related to the problem-solving process. The Whole Brain Thinking approach will help you to find better solutions and make better decisions.

How Do You Collaborate?

'Seek first to understand, then to be understood'—Habit 5 in *The 7 Habits of Highly Effective People* by Dr Stephen R. Covey (1990).

From the preceding paragraphs, it should be clear that you will get the best results by engaging your Whole Brain. Since very few people have equal thinking preferences and skills in all quadrants, you need to collaborate to realise the benefits of Whole Brain Thinking.

All thinking preferences have their own unique value and you can apply them to all situations that require that specific kind of thinking. If you understand how other people prefer to think, it will be easier to adjust your communication style to their 'wavelength' and start collaborating more effectively.

To be straightforward, your thinking preferences reflect the very best version of you. People with different thinking preferences might, with all respect, be a considerably better match for certain tasks and situations. Not reaping the benefits from that knowledge would be a missed opportunity. Put aside your ego and get comfortable with other people's thinking. Show them that you value their way of thinking and learn to appreciate how your thinking preferences are complementary to theirs. That is the essence of habit number 5, as mentioned at the beginning of this section.

The overarching principle in Whole Brain collaboration is trust. People have different thinking preferences, resulting in different approaches to a situation. If you trust that your team is guided by the right intentions and the willingness to create results, you can amplify these differences to generate the advancement the organisation needs to reach the next level.

Further to this, you also need to take different thinking and working preferences from the different generations into account. Members from different generations, but with similar thinking preferences, may express themselves as completely different. Again, 'Seek first to understand, then to be understood'. Embrace the differences; they will make you a better leader.

Listen to others and let yourself be heard.

How Do You Lead?

Are you an authentic leader? How do you know?

Do you know how you lead? Is it in accordance with your thinking preferences? What is the influence of others on your leadership?

In your vertical leadership development, it is important to know where you are now. Are you an expert, an achiever, an individualist or already a strategist? There might (still) be a gap between your thinking preferences and your leadership style. What does that mean for you? It may give you stress, as you are not leading according to your preferences. On the other hand, it may also expand your skills and experience.

When you are in a leadership position, we recommend that you do at least two profiles: one to determine your general thinking preferences (adult profile) and one to determine your leadership style (leadership profile). When you compare the results, you will see whether you lead according to your preferences. In other words, you will discover if you are an authentic leader. When the differences are too big, people will psych it out and, as a consequence, your leadership will be less effective.

We believe that as a leader, you must be able to adjust your leadership style to the ones you lead. You must be able to speak their language as well. If you can tap into their preferences, understand them and make yourself understood, you can create the biggest opportunities for success. In Chapters 4–7, we will further elaborate on each quadrant, but the leadership characteristics of each quadrant can be summarised as follows:

L1	R1
<ul><li>Is an authoritarian</li><li>Is focused and concentrated</li><li>Is the one who cuts the knot</li><li>Wants to have the last word</li><li>Is results driven</li><li>Does it 'the right way' (usually his way)</li></ul>	<ul><li>Is a visionary</li><li>Describes the big picture</li><li>Is future oriented</li><li>Is risk taking</li><li>Is strategic</li><li>Is intuitive</li></ul>
L2	R2
<ul><li>Relies on proven methods</li><li>Likes structure</li><li>Has an eye for details</li><li>Follows rules and regulations</li><li>Is project driven and 'hands-on'</li><li>Is rather risk avoidant</li></ul>	<ul><li>Is team focused</li><li>Prefers consensus</li><li>Is motivating and inspiring</li><li>Is personal and welcoming</li><li>Is sensitive and sentimental</li><li>Is engaging and charming</li></ul>

If you want to improve your skills in a certain quadrant, act more in that quadrant. If it is not your preferred quadrant, working in it may raise your interest and sometimes causes a minor shift in your preferences. Whether or not the latter will happen, at least it will make you a more complete leader.

The Whole Brain Approach

How do you maximise your thinking capacity?

Throughout this chapter, we have talked about the Whole Brain approach. We believe that the key to high-level leadership lies in applying and implementing Whole Brain Thinking into the entire organisation. To make this transformation happen, you need to work on your skills in all the quadrants (next four chapters). You learn to understand that you need others to fill in your blanks, in the same way you are able to fill in theirs.

Forget about the saying 'it's a no-brainer' and replace it with 'it's a Whole Brainer!'

When you grow from an expert to an achiever level, you already make your first step to Whole Brain Thinking. As an expert, you most probably lead from your left brain. You rely on what you know and what is proven and your notion that the rational approach rules. Beware: leading from the left doesn't mean that you also have your strongest preferences there. You might be role-playing!

When you reach the achiever level, you have developed your skills in R2. Because you grow your mindset, it's also possible that you will experience a minor shift in your thinking preferences towards R2. Not a revolutionary one, but more like an evolutionary, gradual one. As an achiever, you engage people into your plans and encourage and motivate them in order to reach their goals.

The next steps in your vertical development as a leader will be towards the individualist and strategist levels. There you will develop your R1 skills. Developing your skills in this quadrant will be easier if you also have your thinking preferences there. You get the big picture and you will be better equipped to develop a vision for your organisation. You now have a mindset that deliberately engages the Whole Brain in the entire organisation. You build on strengths, not weaknesses, and develop the whole organisation and beyond.

Imagine what your organisation would look like if it's engaging the Whole Brain Thinking. Be bold and embrace the future, however unpredictable it may be!

Do the Profiles!

How do you prefer to think?

Well, you have now learned why and how Whole Brain Thinking could help you and your organisation to achieve better results. Can you paint a picture of the future when your organisation embraces Whole Brain Thinking? Can you make an analysis of the facts that support that picture? What does that mean for the bottom line?

When you see the benefits and what it means for the bottom line, how can you structure the process towards the implementation of Whole Brain Thinking? How will the team benefit from this approach? You probably have a rough idea of what your brain profile looks like. That's still a rough idea and maybe a bit biased. If you are serious about your development, we suggest you do the profile to see if your estimations are correct.

As a leader, you can do the leadership profile and discover if your thinking preferences match your leadership style. Many companies are using NBI™ profiles with great success. They also use it as a part of the recruiting process to ensure the best fit for the job. Do you think that knowing the thinking preferences of your whole team would be beneficial? **It's a whole brainer!**

For more information on the profiles, visit our website at: www.wholebrainleader.com

- How do you visualise your organisation when you have successfully integrated Whole Brain Thinking into your daily work?
- What are the real advantages of having Whole Brain Thinking up and running?
- Which steps do you really have to take to make it happen?
- What does Whole Brain Thinking mean for the people involved?

Chapter 4 - L1, The Rational

In this chapter, we discuss what it means to have your thinking preferences in L1. What do the dimensions realist and analyst have in common, and what are the specifics of each dimension?

How does an L1 thinker lead? What are his prejudices or assumptions towards people with thinking preferences in other quadrants? This is the first in a series of four chapters that elaborates on the four different thinking quadrants.

Be aware that you never have all your thinking preferences in just one quadrant or dimension. It is always a mix, and there are always aspects in other quadrants you prefer as well. We're now talking about a **dominant** preference in L1.

Thinking About 'WHAT?'

What is the logic behind your plans? Is it really important? What are the facts and figures?

The L1 thinker is a logical thinker. He wants to work with facts and figures, and builds his cases on solid analysis. His leading question is: WHAT?

What are the facts supporting your idea? What do they mean? What is their impact on other areas? What is our current reality? What are our goals? What are the pitfalls and obstructions preventing us from achieving our goals?

The L1 thinker is focused and wants clarity. He is objective and realistic, doesn't want to make mistakes and searches for the best quality for a reasonable price. He wants to get to the core of the problem and thinks in terms of causes, effects and results. He is not afraid of confrontations. Emotions play a minor role in L1 thinking.

Some clues on how to recognise the Rational L1 thinker are as follows:

- He is performance and results driven.
- He is competitive and has a 'winning' attitude.
- He collects all the relevant information and data before making decisions.
- The decision-making method is fact based. He is not led by emotional considerations and therefore takes an 'objective' stand.
- He is sensitive to a good price/quality ratio.
- He has a no-nonsense approach and an authoritarian appearance.
- He doesn't thrive in an open office environment, and he doesn't want to be distracted.

Do all L1 thinkers think the same? No, in each quadrant, there are two dimensions and there are stark differences between them. L1 has the realist and the analyst dimensions. An L1 thinker with a high preference in the analyst dimension is quite different from an L1 thinker with a high preference in the realist dimension.

The Realist

Can you please show me the facts, so that I can make the right decision?

When you have a thinking preference in the L1-realist dimension, the following words will most probably resonate with you:

- Clarity
- Focus
- Goal setting
- Target
- Concise
- Simple
- Decision
- Facts
- Functional
- Assertive
- Professional
- Logical

The realist wants clarity, quick and concise. He reads the executive summary and uses the facts as a basis for his decisions. He expects the summary to cover the content, but he will double check that as well. He doesn't accept substandard work. He has high expectations, both from himself and from the people around him.

He focuses on what is important, allows no distractions and demands high-quality work. Therefore, he doesn't function well in an open-space office environment. The realist is decisive and direct. People looking for warm and emotionally engaged conversations consider the realist as cold, distant and inflexible.

The Analyst

What will be the consequences for the bottom line?

The analyst differs from the realist, especially when it comes to the speed in which he makes decisions. The realist is focused and makes decisions fast and clear. The analyst wants to dig deeper and takes more time to make a decision. They are both factual and logical thinkers.

Words that will resonate with an analyst are as follows:

- Monitoring
- Analysis
- Finance
- Logic
- Calculations
- Spreadsheets

- If...then
- Examine
- Research
- Diagnosis
- Thorough
- Rational

The analyst excels in Excel. He is the king of the spreadsheet and the prince of pivot tables. Facts, figures and graphs tell him the stories he needs to make justified decisions. After the decisions have been made, the analyst monitors the results. If deviations are detected, adjustments have to be made. He doesn't like unnecessary risks.

The analyst sets priorities. First things first! Like the realist, he sets clear goals and knows what is important and what is merely urgent. He can make that distinction. Goals have to be achieved, no matter what, and there is a strong focus on (financial) performance.

If projects take a wrong turn, there will be an investigation. The analyst will find out *what* went wrong, *why* it went wrong, *how* it could have been avoided and *who* is to blame for it. The analyst has an authoritarian leadership style. If you want things to be done differently, you have to convince him with a watertight analysis based on facts. Assumptions just won't suffice.

How Does the L1, Rational, Lead?

What are the paradigms the L1 thinker lives by? How does he view people with other thinking preferences?

What is it like to be led by the Rational L1 thinker? What are you looking for in a leader? Which traits are important for you? If you're looking for firm leadership, based on a clear view of what has to be done, and you don't mind the distance between the leader and the follower, the L1 leader may be the type you like.

He is focused on results and doesn't beat around the bush. He is direct and clear. He informs you about his expectations and expects that you will not disappoint him. The goals are clear and justified, risks have been minimised and progress will be measured.

You will have key performance indicators set on your tasks, and these will be monitored and discussed regularly. If things go wrong, inform the L1 leader immediately and have the facts available. Be prepared to answer lots of questions and don't irritate him with vague assumptions. He doesn't like 'yes-people' or 'co-dependency'; he prefers (and respects) good and solid arguments. He's not afraid to challenge people and confront them. What the rational likes to call a logical discussion, others might easily see as an argument. The L1 leader needs clear and accurate information in order to make decisions for corrective actions.

Don't expect too many compliments from the L1 leader. Hard work is expected of you and what you're paid for. Don't annoy the L1 leader with chit-chat when you see he's doing important work. He really won't appreciate your invasion of his concentration.

You will find L1 leaders across all industries; however, they tend to flourish where L1 thinking is expected and dominating, for example, in technical and financial professions. When they lead, they feel comfortable relying on these skills. There is another word which is more suitable for leaders who mainly rely on these skills. The word is manager.

People with dominating thinking preferences at the right side of their brain (R1 and R2) often encounter difficulties aligning their thinking preferences with L1 due to his black and white view of the world. Great Whole Brain Leaders (achievers, individualists, strategists), however, will find common wavelengths to communicate effectively with all people, regardless of their thinking preferences.

How Does the L1 Leader See the World?

In the Part 3 of this book, we will describe the leader as a coach. In order to be a great coach, it's essential that you know yourself as well as getting to know the coachee. Both the coach and the coachee have their own thinking preferences.

If you have your dominant thinking preferences in L1, you will probably have some filters towards people with other preferences. In your coaching sessions, you have to be aware of these filters and find ways to neutralise them.

Some will see you as being too authoritarian. That may become an issue when you are coaching. You should be aware of that and pay extra attention to establishing rapport between you and your coachee.

As a leader, if your thinking preferences are dominant in L1, you might have the following prejudices concerning the other quadrants:

The Practical L2 shares your love for logical thinking. You appreciate his loyalty, punctuality and perseverance. He gets things done. On the other hand, you may have some second thoughts about his attachment to the status quo. Change is a big issue for the Practical L2 and that may become a source of irritation.

The Relational R2 is someone you appreciate for his ability to cheer and motivate other people—something you're not very well known for. When he believes in your mission and goals, you have a strong ally. However, the Relational R2 is also someone who resists change. You sometimes have to dive into emotions in order to convince him of the necessity of the proposed changes.

For you, the Experimental R1 is finally someone who feels comfortable with change. Maybe a bit too comfortable? He has a clear vision of the future and sees the big picture. The downside is that people with these thinking preferences usually have a lot of ideas, but not the same enthusiasm to follow up on them. You might consider the majority of his ideas as crazy and unrealistic, but there are some diamonds in-between that you could polish. You two can be a strong combination when you agree that the Experimental R1 takes care of the diverging (quantity) phase and you, the Realistic, of the converging (quality) phase of creative thinking.

- If you were an L1 leader, how would you overcome your prejudices towards the other thinking preferences?
- What will be your strategy to step up to Whole Brain Thinking?

Chapter 5 – L2, The Practical

In this chapter, we discuss what it means to have a thinking preference in L2. What do the dimensions preserver and organiser have in common, and what are the differences between these dimensions?

How does an L2 thinker lead? What are his prejudices or assumptions towards people with thinking preferences in the other quadrants?

Remember that you never have all your thinking preferences in just one quadrant or dimension. It's always a mix and there are always aspects you like in other quadrants as well. In this chapter, we are talking about a **dominant** preference in L2.

Another thing to keep in mind while we are going through these chapters is that we discuss the **preferences,** not the skills. They may be the same, but that is not a given.

Thinking About 'HOW?'

> *How have we solved this issue before? What were the results?*

Like the L1, the L2 is a logical thinker. However, there are quite some differences between these quadrants. The L2 thinker is concerned with well-proven systems, methods and structures. His leading question is: HOW?

How can we plan this project? How can we structure the activities? How can we work in a safe and efficient manner? How did we do it in the past? How can we ensure that we will finish in time? How do we arrange sufficient support and resources?

The L2 thinker is focused on getting things done. He asks the practical questions in order to execute his detailed plans. He is action oriented, but doesn't jump in without being prepared. He likes to take sufficient time for these preparations and relies on experience. He is hands-on and disciplined, and expects the same from the people he works and shares his life with.

Some clues by which you can recognise someone with a thinking preference in L2, the Practical, are as follows:

- In meetings, he will show up on time and is well prepared.
- His desk is clean and organised—also inside his cabinets.
- He has a tendency to be a perfectionist and will elaborate on the details.
- He will probably label people. He thinks in categories and structures.
- He is the one finding flaws in otherwise 'brilliant' plans.
- He doesn't like change. 'We have always done it like this, and it always worked out fine. So why should we change?'
- He likes to have routine in his daily life.

Like with all quadrants, the L2 has two different dimensions: the preserver and the organiser. The preferences can be equally divided over both dimensions, but you can also have stronger preferences in a particular one. This means that not all L2 thinkers can be labelled the same. For the L2 thinker, that can be a shame (because he likes to categorise) as well as a blessing (because he might like to dive deep into the details). Again, this depends on the dimension he is most connected with.

The Preserver

> *We have done this before. We have the right systems in place to do it again, so why should we change our approach?*

When you have strong thinking preferences in the L2 preserver dimension, the following words might resonate with you:

- Order
- Discipline
- Punctual
- Proven
- Loyal
- Experience
- Safe
- Rules
- Regulations
- Method
- Traditional
- Structured

The preserver wants discipline and order. He is a tower of strength, trustworthy and loyal, towards his friends, co-workers and employer. He relies on experience. He knows what has worked before and what hasn't. If you suggest something new, he will not be very enthusiastic. It means that he has to think through all the consequences of this new idea, and that implies investing valuable time in something with an uncertain outcome. 'Why should one do that, when there are proven alternatives?'

The Organiser

Goal? Check!—Strategy? Check!—Plan? Check!—Okay, let's implement!

In the L1 quadrant, the realist and analyst differ in the speed with which they like to make decisions. Something similar is also the case when you compare the preserver and the organiser. The organiser is more action oriented, whereas the preserver focuses more on control. For both the preserver and the organiser, VUCA is a real threat.

When you have thinking preferences in the L2 organiser dimension, the following words might resonate with you:

- Control
- Action
- Hands-on
- To-Do list
- Schedule
- Planning
- Supervision
- Milestones
- Progress
- Process
- Persist
- Endure

The organiser likes to get things done. He likes to plan every step in the process and connect other underlying plans to the main plan. He prepares the resources and supervises the process. He prefers to work with systems, to-do lists, schedules and checklists. When the going gets tough, the organiser gets going! Giving up is not in his dictionary! Results are important for him.

Once you are clear about the organisational goals, you definitely want the organiser to design the plans to realise them. The R1 may have brilliant ideas, the L1 can filter the best and set goals, but the organiser is the one who will work systematically towards achieving them!

How Does the L2, Practical, Lead?

If you like a structured approach, working according to plan and getting to results, L2, the Practical may be your leader of choice.

What is it like to be led by the L2 leader?

He has a stable and traditional way of leading. He is very well structured, organised and professional. His focus is more on results than on people. If you are inexperienced, but hard working, you can learn a lot from the L2 supervisor. The L2 leader expects you to be on time and well prepared. He doesn't like people cutting corners.

When you're working on a project supervised by an L2 leader with strong thinking preferences in the organiser dimension, he can immediately inform you what has been done, where you are in the project and what remains. He keeps track of the resources and what needs to be ordered. He is the spider in the web.

If you're more experienced, you may at times feel micromanaged by the practical leader. He doesn't give much freedom in the way the work is executed. There are proven methods, and they have to be adhered to. If overtime is needed to get things done, he expects everyone to take his share. You must have very good reasons if you want your private matters to prevail over work.

You will find L2 leaders across all industries, but they thrive best in functions where a sharp eye for detail is needed, and where work has to be executed in a reliable and structured way. You will find many L2 leaders in supervising roles. When you look at their stage of development, you will most likely recognise the expert (see Chapter 1).

How Does the L2 Leader See the World?

When, as a leader, you want to coach the ones you lead, it's of paramount importance to know yourself as well as getting to know your coachee. In Part 3 of this book, we elaborate on the leader as a coach and connect that to the thinking preferences of the ones involved.

How can I survive the chaotic world we're living in?

If you happen to have your dominant thinking preferences in L2, you will probably have certain filters towards people with thinking preferences in other quadrants. When you do your coaching, be aware of these filters and find ways to neutralise them.

The L2 Practical thinker likes to depend on structure, systems and order. He needs to be in control. The L2 leader plays by the rules. He's probably well prepared when he starts his coaching sessions. He will have a step-by-step approach. The conversations can therefore be rather predictable.

Let's assume that you have your dominant thinking preferences in L2. By some you will be seen as a micromanager and inflexible. That may become quite an issue when you're coaching others. Be aware that it's not about you, and how you do your work, but about the coachee, and how he finds his way in his development. Sometimes you have to take sideways to reach your goals.

Because of your thinking preferences in L2, you may have the following prejudices towards the other quadrants:

The Rational L1 is a logical and realistic thinker, so you don't have to be too sensitive to feelings. You appreciate his clarity and thorough factual thinking. He sets clear goals and targets. On the other hand, he does have quite an ego and finds it hard to admit when he's wrong. People may say you're a micromanager, but in your opinion, the Rational L1 has invented it. 'It's his way or the highway'.

The Relational R2 is someone you appreciate, because he manages to motivate the team to execute your plans and he has a good way of dealing with people in general; he's a collaborative person. On the other hand, he can also be quite stubborn when he thinks that the plans are not right for him and his team. He can inhibit progress. He also tends to be overly sensitive and is weak on discipline. The human factor can be rather irritating.

The Experimental R1 is resourceful; he can generate many solutions to problems and find order in chaos. He also respects other people's points of view. However, sometimes you get a bit overwhelmed by all these new ideas. Why doesn't he follow up before generating another bunch of new ideas. It seems as if he is not interested in details. For you, that's his pitfall, because you know that the devil is in the details.

When you are aware of how your own thinking influences the way you perceive others, you will figure out how you can benefit from each other's strengths. These are the necessary steps to start using the Whole Brain. The learning takes place outside of your comfort zone. In other words, you learn the most when you practise and adapt to the other thinking preferences as well. Experiencing the strengths of the other quadrants will make you a more complete leader. It will help you to develop yourself and others towards the next level of leadership.

▶ If you were an L2 leader, how would you overcome your prejudices towards the other thinking preferences?

▶ What will be your strategic plan to experience the Whole Brain?

Chapter 6 - R2, The Relational

After having discussed the logical side of the brain, it's now time to discover the right side. As we've mentioned before, we often talk about the left and right sides of the brain, but as we collect more insights into how the brain actually works, we now know that these thinking activities are not necessarily happening at the physical left or right side of the brain. The activities are spread around the whole brain and more or less act in clusters. In order not to make things too complicated, we have decided to keep talking about left- and right-side thinking.

In this chapter, we will have a look into the 'people-quadrant' R2, also known as the relational. What does it mean to have strong thinking preferences in R2? What do the two dimensions, socialiser and empathiser, have in common, and what are their specific preferences within this quadrant?

How does the Relational R2 lead? How does he judge people with strong thinking preferences in the other quadrants, and what are his assumptions about them?

Thinking About 'WHO?'

Who is involved in these plans? What does that mean for them?

The Relational R2 thinker is concerned with people. He never forgets the human element. People are more important than tasks. His leading question is: WHO?

Who wants to collaborate? Who wants to take part in this team? Who will be affected by this project? Who wants to get together and discuss this issue?

The R2 thinker is a team player. People are the key to success. Taking care of the team will help them to succeed. The R2 is an intuitive thinker. If things don't 'feel' right to him, you will have a hard time to get him on board. He is enthusiastic about ideas and he doesn't mind to add his own insights to them, but he's careful when those ideas mean change. If that's the case, he definitely wants to know the effects the changes will have on his team.

Maybe you recognise the following Relational R2 traits:

- He gathers people around him and communicates easily.
- He has an instinctive approach and relies more on feelings than on facts.
- Values are important. People must be respected for who they are and how they think.
- He is a good listener.
- He tends to give positive feedback.
- He believes in group dynamics.
- He likes an open-door policy.

Within the R2 quadrant, we also have two dimensions: the socialiser and empathiser. As with the other quadrants, they have distinctive characteristics.

The Socialiser

How can we approach this issue together? Who wants to share his ideas with the team?

The socialiser likes to work in groups and values the ideas of others. He wants to know what other people think before he makes his decisions. Group dynamics are important, and so is a good atmosphere. He senses when the mood changes.

If you are a socialiser, the following words will most probably resonate with you:

- Networking
- Teamwork
- Motivating
- Together
- Sharing
- Expressive
- People
- Passion
- Interpersonal
- Consensus
- Tolerant
- Moral standards

The socialiser likes to meet new people and to mingle. He is open and likes to entertain others. People feel comfortable talking to him. He likes to find out which people are the best fit for which projects and wants to compose teams accordingly.

The Empathiser

With the dimensions in the L1 quadrant, there were differences in the speed of decision-making. In the L2 quadrant, there were differences in the desire to take action. The major difference between the socialiser and empathiser is in the number of people they prefer to work with.

The socialiser likes to work with larger groups, whereas the empathiser prefers the smaller groups or even one-on-one contacts.

Words that may resonate with the empathiser are as follows:

- Caring
- Nurturing
- Listening
- Helping
- Encouraging
- Cheering
- Service
- Adding value to others
- Intuition
- Relationship
- Sensitive

The empathiser is willing to lend an ear. He listens empathically. He takes feelings seriously and helps to find solutions when you're in trouble. He is kind and understanding.

How Does the R2, Relational, Lead?

How can my team survive the chaotic world we're living in?

Do you feel the warmth of the relational leader? From what you have read about the R2 so far, you can probably paint a picture of the Relational R2 as a leader.

The R2 leader values teamwork and cooperation and finds it important to have all on board. He appreciates interaction with others and wants to hear what's keeping them busy. When he has decisions to make, he prefers to involve others and reach consensus.

He enjoys group dynamics and is eager to share information. Feelings are more important than facts. In problem-solving, it's important for him that the human aspects are being addressed and respected. Although most people claim to live by their values, they play a significant role for the Relational.

When going through change processes, the emotional side of the relational can inhibit the progress. People with other dominant thinking preferences need to respect his emotions about the process or else change might become extremely difficult. On the other hand, if you have convinced the R2 leader why the change is important for his team, he will probably support the plans and work hard to get buy-in from other stakeholders.

If the atmosphere changes, he will usually notice this first and take action. In order to keep the team spirit high, the R2 leader likes to organise social gatherings and events, where he makes himself available to the team.

You can find R2 leaders across many different industries, but they will truly thrive in functions where people, groups and teams play a major role.

Leaders with an R2 thinking preference understand that collaboration is essential to achieve goals. If they also have supporting preferences or skills in L1 and/or L2, you may have found an achiever (see Chapter 1). An achiever achieves goals because he understands the power of collaboration and enjoys leveraging this power.

How Does the R2 Leader See the World?

To take the next step in leadership, being a coach to the ones you lead, you have to know how you perceive the world from your thinking preferences. If you want to understand the ones you lead and coach, you first have to understand yourself. Embrace all thinking preferences for what they are. In essence, they are not positive nor negative. It's what you make of it. In coaching, you need to be open to all thinking preferences.

Let's assume that you have your dominant thinking preferences in R2. By some, you will be seen as too soft and too attached to comfort. In coaching the ones you lead, you will probably be able to create an atmosphere of trust, which will make it easier to establish rapport. On the other hand, you may find it difficult to get out of your, and your coachee's, comfort zone. In coaching, it's important to stretch your boundaries.

Because of your thinking preferences in R2, you may have the following prejudices towards other quadrants:

You like the Rational L1 for his clarity and his well thought through decisions. He is strong in fact finding and analysis. Unfortunately, his decisions are primarily fact based. In your opinion, he ignores the human factor and lacks emotional intelligence. It's very hard to have a good conversation about feelings, he's just too clinical and calculating. His ego is too big, and you don't like his authoritarian (leadership) style.

The Practical L2 creates stability, he's loyal and gets things done. He is concerned about safety and doesn't like to shake things up. On the other hand, he tends to be bossy and, like the Rational L1, lacks emotional intelligence. He micromanages and is inflexible, but worst of all, he puts tasks over people!

With the Experimental R1, you can have fun. He's an informal kind of person, creative and generates lots of ideas. If you want to know what the world would look like in five to ten years, he is the one to paint that picture. He's an intuitive kind of thinker. Unfortunately, he's also the one causing restlessness with all his ideas that lead to change. He is risk taking and he can't be trusted to follow up on decisions that have been made. He is too easily bored with the status quo.

You see that having different thinking preferences influences the way you see others. There's always the danger of judging others, with your own dominant thinking preferences as your reference.

A great step towards Whole Brain Leadership is to understand that in certain circumstances, other thinking preferences are more suitable.

Bringing the best of all worlds together increases the adaptability of the team, which is necessary to deal with VUCA. When the leader with an R2 preference understands that, he can bring himself and coach his team towards the next level.

- ▶ If you were an R2 thinker, how would you overcome your prejudices towards the other thinking preferences?
- ▶ How can you involve your team in Whole Brain Thinking?
- ▶ Who are the ones resisting change the most? How are you going to help them to adapt to VUCA?

Chapter 7 – R1, The Experimental

When we talk about thinking out of the box, we refer to the R1 thinking preferences. In this chapter, we explore what it means to have your thinking preferences in R1, also known as the experimental.

We will paint a picture on what the two dimensions within the quadrant, strategist and imagineer, mean. What do they have in common and where do they differ?

What does an R1 Experimental leader look like? How does he lead? How does he appreciate people with strong thinking preferences in the other quadrants? What are his feelings towards them?

Thinking About 'WHY?'

Why are we doing this? Can't we do it in a better way?

The R1 thinker is the risk taker, who challenges the status quo. He prefers the big picture and visualises what the future may look like. He likes to connect seemingly unrelated ideas to create something new.

Why do we do the things we do? Why should this be the only solution? Why don't we use these solutions in other problem areas as well? Why don't we work towards a better future? Why should we be afraid of VUCA?

These are just a few questions an Experimental R1 might ask.

People with strong R1 thinking preferences are unconventional thinkers. They don't need a structure to make connections between unrelated issues. They jump from one idea to the other. When you start to understand one idea, the R1 thinker has already generated five others.

Is it new? 'Hmm, might be interesting'. Does it involve change? 'Tell me more!' The experimental thinker likes to combine ideas to build a picture. He is future oriented, often skips the details and definitely challenges the status quo.

Some clues to recognise R1, the Experimental, are as follows:

- He's always on the lookout for new adventures.
- He thinks in possibilities, not in problems.
- He listens to his inner voice. Facts and analysis are less important.
- He thinks in pictures and metaphors.
- He's a visionary.
- He adores change and transformation.
- He is comfortable with chaos and has the ability to juggle with many tasks simultaneously.

Within the R1 quadrant, we distinguish the strategist and imagineer dimensions. The strategist connects past and future and looks at the **big** picture, whereas the imagineer thinks in pictures for everything and dreams up new intuitive schemes.

The Strategist

*What does the world look like five years from now?
Are we ready for that?*

The strategist has a strong vision and a horizon far into the future, for which he likes to make predictions. He challenges the present and likes to design scenarios. He explores new options and possibilities, and is often perceived as a bit restless. He is able and willing to look through other people's eyes for different angles, but don't bother him with the nitty-gritty details.

If you are a strategist, the following words will probably resonate with you:

- Future
- Scenario
- Vision
- Strategic
- Big picture
- Change
- Transformation
- Connections
- New
- Unfamiliar
- Challenge
- Synergy

The strategist likes to connect the past with the future. He likes to generate ideas from a wide variety of insights and experiences. Risk is never a show-stopper; it's part of the game. The strategist often asks challenging questions in order to move on and create something new and better.

The Imagineer

Can you paint me a picture? Which metaphors can we use?

The imagineer is very different from the strategist; in fact, he is different from all other dimensions as well, and that's exactly what he likes to be—unorthodox. It's often hard to get him to obey rules and regulations (he has his own set). He likes to create.

If you are an imagineer, the following words will probably resonate with you:

- Pictures
- Inner voice
- Meditation
- Aha moment
- Dream
- Drawing
- Metaphor
- Unorthodox
- Chaotic
- Unstructured
- New
- Exciting
- Fantasy
- Intuition
- Imagine
- Draw

If you're looking for fresh ideas, don't forget to pay the imagineer a visit.

How Does the R1, Experimental, Lead?

Which new and innovative ways of doing business can we think of? Where will they lead us to?

If your leader happens to be an R1 Experimental, and you happen to like stability, security and predictability, you may have a hard time. If, on the other hand, you're looking for a leader who thrives in a VUCA world, you may be lucky. You **may** be lucky, because we're talking about **thinking preferences,** not **skills.** If he has the R1 skills as well, then you have found the right leader!

Nevertheless, he should realise that he needs to include people with different thinking preferences in his team as well; he cannot do it all on his own. Luckily, the R1 leader doesn't cling to his authority and is more than willing to share.

The experimental leader likes strategic sessions, but will easily be bored when it comes to the details. He is enthusiastic about evaluating the future, and when he believes in an idea, he is willing to take risks. Unfortunately, he is not the one to follow through on the ideas. Therefore, it is necessary to have the other quadrants in play as well.

For the Rational L1 follower: take the ideas of the R1 leader with you, analyse the facts, do your calculations and share your feedback with him. It's best to come up with a top three of the best ideas. The L2 Practical can figure out how to realise the ideas, and thus promote them into innovations.

For the L2 follower: when the decisions have been made on which ideas need to be worked out in detail, use your skills to actually fabricate the plans. R1 will probably put that at the end of his agenda. Then provide him with an executive summary. Don't make it too long and detailed, because you will lose him if you do.

For the R2 follower: the R1 leader is not authoritarian. He just likes to challenge people and situations, and does that by asking a lot of questions. If you have issues about what the new plans mean for your team, be open with him. He is also open for your suggestions. Tell him about your challenges, and he will help you find solutions, but don't nag. The future is important to him, and so are the transformations necessary to deal with that future. Assist your team in going through the changes, and help them to embrace them, instead of resisting the inevitable.

You can find R1 leaders across many different industries, but when the organisation is too traditional, and even resisting change as well, he will not stay long. He thrives in functions where he can share his ideas, and where his vision of the future is needed. He is in his element when he can transform businesses and challenge the status quo.

Leaders with an R1 thinking preference, in particular the strategists, are most likely to embrace the journey into Whole Brain Leadership. They will feel comfortable at the individualist and strategist levels. They don't want to fit in; they want to stand out!

How Does the R1 Leader See the World?

What has the future got to offer and what can we do to reap the opportunities?

If you have your dominant thinking preferences in R1, you will probably have no problems getting people out of their comfort zones. When coaching, be aware that your coachees may have different thinking preferences, and they need some guidance when they're going too far away from their familiar grounds. They will need more structure than you do, and as a coach, you should provide that. Also, bear in mind that people with thinking preferences in R1 are the only ones that really embrace change. The others are less confident with it. Adjust your pace a bit!

Let's assume that you have your dominant thinking preferences in R1. You may be seen as being fun to work with, but many see you as the one that is continuously changing his mind, and who doesn't follow up on decisions made. In coaching the ones you lead, you are the best in assisting your coachees to visualise what they discover, but you also have to take care to create a safe and secure atmosphere. That may prove to be a challenge for you.

Because of your thinking preferences in R1, you may have the following prejudices towards other quadrants:

The things you appreciate about the L1 are: his orientation towards the future, his analytical skills and his ability to make clear decisions. On the other hand, where's the fun? He is too realistic, and he doesn't like to think out of the box. Things have to be proven with facts and analysis. What's wrong with gut feelings? Furthermore, he's authoritarian and his ego is too big.

The nice thing about the L2 Practical is his drive to get things done and his reliability. He can realise ideas and transform them into innovations. What you probably dislike about the L2 is his resistance to change. You can hardly call him flexible, and he bores you with his details. For you, he's too formal, and he relies too much on old beliefs, rules and regulations. You wish that he would take some more risks.

The Relational R2 thinker acts on intuition as well, just like you. He involves others in problem-solving and is easily approachable. In your opinion, the R2 thinker is a bit too concerned about his people. That makes him resistant to change as well. 'He shouldn't be thinking about his team so much; let them develop their own thinking too. Maybe that will help them to get out of their comfort zones as well'. His emotions often confine new ideas.

Using the strengths of the other thinking preferences will help the R1 Experimental to realise his strategies and deal with VUCA. He has to respect other people's thinking preferences to get all of them on board. Sometimes he needs to practise patience in order to be successful.

The R1 Experimental can play a major role in coaching the others to grow vertically and adapt to VUCA.

▶ How can you get all the others, with their different thinking preferences, to believe in your vision of the future?

- How will you handle other people's natural resistance to change?
- Which strengths of each quadrant/dimension can you utilise to deal with VUCA?

Chapter 8 – Whole Brain Thinking

In the previous chapters, we have examined and described thinking preferences in four quadrants and eight dimensions. In this chapter, we will wrap this up in four tables, painting a picture of how people with thinking preferences in different quadrants perceive each other. The tables will not give you all the details; that's simply impossible. Instead, they give you insights into how people may perceive each other based on their preferences and those of the others.

A caution we have emphasised in the previous chapters is that you always have a mix of preferences distributed over the four quadrants and eight dimensions. This is the same for the four tables we give you. Think of it as the perceptions of people with dominant thinking preferences in a certain quadrant.

Why do we wrap all this up in the tables? Is it just nice and interesting to know how you are perceived by others, and how you perceive people with other thinking preferences? Yes, of course, it's nice and interesting, but that's not the point. For us, it's important that you take your next step in thinking. Do not only use your own dominant thinking preferences, but explore the others as well. Jump from one quadrant to the other when you're solving problems, thinking of strategies, making decisions, executing your tasks or coaching your team.

Here you start practising Whole Brain Thinking, an important step towards Whole Brain Leadership. How others see you, and how you see others, depends on:

- the nature of your relationship
- your thinking preferences and those of others
- the environment and situation
- your level of development

We will start from the perspective of the different thinking preferences, and after that you will be able to make educated guesses on how you're being seen by your boss, co-workers, clients, spouse or children.

When You Have Your Thinking Preferences in L1, the Rational

You think logic is king. Try creativity for a change.

How people with thinking preferences in the various quadrants see the L1 thinker is listed in Table 8.1.

We've not only considered the other quadrants, but also people with their dominant thinking preferences in the same quadrant as you, because you also have to deal with people with roughly the same thinking preferences as you.

Sometimes your thinking preferences lead to the best results, but in other situations, you can better leave some of the responsibility and ownership to the others. It may well be that pushing your thinking forward will limit progress. You should tolerate and comprehend other thinking preferences and allow them their piece of action as well.

Table 8.1: How Others See the Rational L1

	Pros	Cons
The Rational L1	<ul><li>His rational and logical approach.</li><li>His focus on what's important.</li><li>He gets straight to the point.</li><li>He sets clear goals.</li><li>He doesn't show unnecessary emotions.</li></ul>	<ul><li>We're both competitive and there can only be one winner.</li><li>He always wants to have the final say.</li><li>He can't admit when he is wrong.</li></ul>
The Practical L2	<ul><li>He's a logical and realistic thinker.</li><li>He makes clear decisions.</li><li>He sets clear goals/targets.</li><li>His clear focus makes planning easier.</li><li>He conducts detailed analysis.</li></ul>	<ul><li>He wants to be right about everything.</li><li>His ego is too big.</li><li>He's authoritarian.</li><li>He's a micromanager.</li></ul>
The Relational R2	<ul><li>He doesn't take unnecessary risks.</li><li>His communication is clear and coherent.</li><li>His decisions are well thought trough.</li><li>He's decisive.</li></ul>	<ul><li>He lacks emotional intelligence.</li><li>He always wants to be right.</li><li>He's calculating and clinical.</li><li>He's authoritarian.</li><li>His ego is too big.</li></ul>

(Continued)

	Pros	Cons
The Experimental R1	<ul><li>He's future oriented.</li><li>He can analyse my ideas.</li><li>He sets realistic goals.</li><li>He can help realising my ideas.</li></ul>	<ul><li>He's too critical.</li><li>He isn't original.</li><li>He tends to be inflexible.</li><li>He's authoritarian.</li><li>He's sterile (no fun).</li></ul>

As an L1 leader, you worship facts, so it must be easy to understand the fact that there are other effective ways of thinking too. You focus on results. It's also a fact that when you apply Whole Brain Thinking, the results will improve. Embrace it and build on the specific qualities of all involved. Don't nag about the perceived weaknesses of others. Focus on their strengths. Although it may not be your strongest quality, and probably outside your comfort zone, exercise patience.

You should make the best use of other people's thinking preferences and practise your thinking in the other quadrants and dimensions as well.

Maybe you have read Dr Edward de Bono's *Six Thinking Hats* (1985). He described six thinking roles and directions, depicting them as six hats with different colours. By consciously applying different thinking roles to decision-making processes, the decisions made improve considerably.

More or less in line with that principle, you can make a training programme for yourself to deliberately develop your thinking in the other quadrants. Some suggestions for the L1 thinker could be as follows.

In L2:

- Plan a business meeting from start to finish. Go through all the details.

- Create and follow a long-term training schedule for your personal and professional development. Which steps will you take, when will you do that, which resources do you need and what are the milestones? How do you keep track?

In R2:

- Choose three co-workers and find out what is the most important to them in life.

- Organise a party to celebrate a team accomplishment.

- Give a speech in which you highlight the successes of the others and don't mention your own role.

In R1:

- Create a mind map in which you paint a picture of what the organisation looks like in 10 years from now, where Whole Brain Thinking is the norm.

- Close the door of your office, meditate for 15 minutes and do nothing else than listening to your thoughts. Set a timer and, after 15 minutes, create a mind map including everything you can recall from your meditation. Don't suppress silly thoughts.

Table 8.2: How Others See the Practical L2

	Pros	Cons
The Rational L1	<ul><li>He's a logical thinker.</li><li>He's loyal, disciplined and punctual.</li><li>He sets up realistic plans and gets them executed.</li><li>He's organised, supervises and perseveres.</li></ul>	<ul><li>He resists change.</li><li>He's too detail oriented.</li><li>He puts too much emphasis on experienced people and proven methods.</li><li>He's too dependent on his 'old' methods. Not open towards shifting realities.</li></ul>
The Practical L2	<ul><li>He's well prepared and stable.</li><li>He's disciplined.</li><li>He's loyal.</li><li>He's in control.</li><li>He's experienced.</li></ul>	<ul><li>He spends too much time fighting change.</li><li>He's a micromanager.</li><li>He tends to be inflexible.</li></ul>
The Relational R2	<ul><li>He's stable.</li><li>He's loyal.</li><li>He's cautious.</li><li>He's organised.</li><li>He's correct.</li></ul>	<ul><li>Tasks are more important to him than people.</li><li>He's bossy.</li><li>He's a micromanager.</li><li>He tends to be inflexible.</li><li>He lacks emotional intelligence.</li></ul>
The Experimental R1	<ul><li>He transforms ideas into projects.</li><li>He's reliable.</li><li>He gets things done.</li><li>He's experienced.</li><li>He's practical.</li></ul>	<ul><li>He resist change.</li><li>He's too detail oriented.</li><li>He's too formal.</li><li>He relies too much on experience.</li><li>He's afraid of risks.</li></ul>

When You Have Your Thinking Preferences in L2, the Practical

Sometimes 'uncommon sense' is more appropriate.

How people with thinking preferences in the various quadrants see the L2 thinker is listed in Table 8.2.

An L2 leader depends on structure, systems and order. He needs to be in control. Step-by-step planning gives him security. But is it really a safe approach?

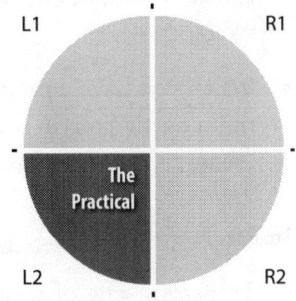

It would be an important paradigm shift for the L2 leader to discover that nature itself also gives structure to everything, even chaos. If you have your thinking preferences in L2, and have not yet started to study this, we suggest you to try to find patterns in nature, the meaning behind those patterns and how they became apparent.

If you comprehend the structure of nature and what it means for your professional environment, you may find that adapting to changes is a proven method as well. That will help you to thrive in a VUCA world. Adapting to change is usually safer than fighting it.

Let's have a look at what a training programme for the L2, Practical, leader could include.

In L1:

- Challenge your routine. Write a new proposal for the improvement of one of your working methods, based only on facts. Make it short and to the point. Skip the details.

- In the next important meeting that you will attend, you have to sell Whole Brain Thinking. You will get 5 minutes to convince the attendees. Prepare a speech, based on facts and analysis, resulting in the support of the team.

In R2:

- Have a one-on-one conversation with one of your team members and tell him what you appreciate about him. Prepare yourself and be genuine. Repeat this exercise until you realise its value.

- When you have a project to prepare, invite your team in and let them participate in the preparations. Don't interfere too much. Observe how 'the chaos' develops into order.

In R1:

- Transform one of your step-by-step project plans into a mind map. Insert pictures for every main topic. After having finished your mind map, tell your team the story of what the future, after completion of the project, looks like. Don't forget the WIIFM (What's In It For Me) for them.

- In order to overcome your resistance to change, write down a positive consequence of the change for each objection you have regarding that particular change. Be the angel's advocate for a change.

When You Have Your Thinking Preferences in R2, the Relational

How people with thinking preferences in the various quadrants see the R2 thinker is listed in Table 8.3.

How can you really help the people you lead?

For the R2 leader, it will be a major paradigm shift to discover that hanging on to stability and rejecting change will not bring any

Table 8.3: How Others See the Relational R2

	Pros	Cons
The Rational L1	<ul><li>He usually is cooperative.</li><li>He can mobilise people.</li><li>He is inspiring.</li><li>He detects mood changes at an early stage.</li><li>He's strong in networking.</li></ul>	<ul><li>He's too concerned about people.</li><li>He doesn't consider the facts.</li><li>He relies too much on feelings.</li><li>He is too sentimental.</li><li>Consensus is important to him.</li></ul>
The Practical L2	<ul><li>He can motivate people into executing plans.</li><li>He is supportive.</li><li>He respects the status quo.</li><li>He can build functional teams.</li></ul>	<ul><li>He puts too much emphasis on people.</li><li>He's weak on discipline.</li><li>He gives too much freedom to those he leads.</li><li>Too much talking when 'walking' is needed.</li></ul>
The Relational R2	<ul><li>He is good with people.</li><li>He is a strong communicator.</li><li>He is collaborative.</li><li>He is easily approachable.</li><li>He keeps the spirit high.</li></ul>	<ul><li>He's too noisy and outgoing.</li><li>He spends too much time on one person.</li><li>He's easy to manipulate.</li><li>He's too much of a pleaser.</li></ul>

(*Continued*)

	👍 Pros	👎 Cons
The Experimental R1	• He acts on gut feeling. • He involves others in problem-solving. • He likes to share (ideas). • He is easily approachable.	• He doesn't like change. • He is too concerned about his people to see the big picture. • Emotions often confine new ideas. • He wants to stay (and play) in his comfort zone.

security to his team. Adapting to change will. In order to provide the highest level of security possible, he must overcome his aversion to change.

If you happen to be an R2 leader, you should consider putting more emphasis on the unique strengths of each team member and choosing the fittest for each task. That will help them to deal with VUCA.

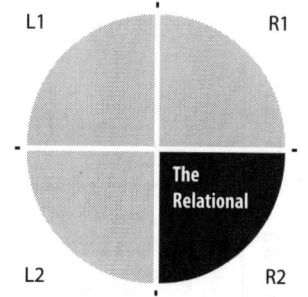

How could you train yourself in the other quadrants when you are an R2 leader?

In L1:

- Give a bad performing employee a factual evaluation. Limit your eye contact, list the items to improve upon and share the consequences when he doesn't improve.

- Evaluate a new idea purely on facts and what it means for the financial bottom line. Ignore the human factor.

In L2:

- Set up a formal 360° assessment schedule for your team and plan the dates when you will have your feedback meetings. You can use the questionnaire from Chapter 2.
- Read your quality management manual and check if the processes are still up to date.

In R1:

- Organise a creative thinking session with your team in which you have to come up with at least five viable ways to introduce Whole Brain Thinking into your organisation.
- Together with your team, create a picture of your organisation in five years from now. Use all kinds of materials. The result should be exhibited and explained to others. What's the story?

When You Have Your Thinking Preferences in R1, the Experimental

Ready for an experiment? Try a different thinking preference.

How people with thinking preferences in the various quadrants see the R1 thinker is listed in Table 8.4.

R1 is the only quadrant where change is embraced. For people with thinking preferences in this quadrant, it can be hard to understand why people with other thinking preferences put so much energy in rejecting change. VUCA is not chaotic for the R1 thinker; it's just the reality to which you have to adapt.

Table 8.4: How Others See the Experimental R1

	Pros	Cons
The Rational L1	<ul><li>He can see the big picture.</li><li>He has a vision of the future.</li><li>He can generate lots of ideas.</li><li>He explores uncharted territory.</li></ul>	<ul><li>He takes too many risks.</li><li>He is zigzagging in his thinking.</li><li>Too many ideas are crazy and unrealistic.</li><li>He is a daydreamer.</li></ul>
The Practical L2	<ul><li>He can generate lots of ideas.</li><li>He is resourceful.</li><li>He takes various angles when assessing situations.</li><li>He finds order in chaos.</li></ul>	<ul><li>His ideas are often unrealistic.</li><li>He's disruptive.</li><li>He doesn't appreciate details.</li><li>He is unstructured.</li><li>He takes too many risks.</li></ul>
The Relational R2	<ul><li>He's creative.</li><li>He can generate lots of ideas.</li><li>He's fun to work with.</li><li>He has an informal style.</li><li>He respects other people's point of view.</li></ul>	<ul><li>He wants too many changes.</li><li>He takes too many risks.</li><li>He is too focused on the big picture.</li><li>He 'forgets' about decisions that have been made.</li></ul>
The Experimental R1	<ul><li>He can generate lots of ideas.</li><li>He's a visual thinker.</li><li>He welcomes change.</li><li>He's unorthodox.</li></ul>	<ul><li>He's a daydreamer.</li><li>He's too occupied with the future.</li><li>He's too chaotic.</li><li>He doesn't follow through.</li></ul>

One could easily conclude that the R1 leader embraces this constantly changing world. Most of the times they are energetic indeed, and they come up with lots of ideas. On the other hand, they also get a bit frustrated every now and then by all the resistance they have to overcome.

In order to make his life easier, the R1 leader should also walk in the shoes of the other quadrants. For him, we have made a small selection of training exercises as well.

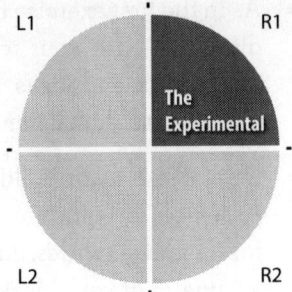

If you are an R1 leader, you have probably thought of some exercises already.

In L1:

- Choose three ideas you have generated recently. Find real facts that support your ideas. Make a thorough analysis!

- Make yourself really uncomfortable with the following exercise. Rearrange your office. Make it minimal and functional, remove all clutter and vivid decorations (apart from those showing your achievements).

In L2:

- Take one of your 'big pictures' of the future, for example, how your organisation has adopted Whole Brain Leadership. Fill in all the details (resources, meetings, financial issues, etc.) for the coming quarter, and design a step-by-step plan to reach your goals.

- Take your quality management handbook, and check which procedures remain valid and which need to change because of the previous exercise.

In R2:

- As in the first exercise from L2, take your 'big picture' again, and discuss it with your team. Listen empathically to their objections, fears, and ideas. Don't judge, defend your ideas or coach the persons. Just listen very well to what they have to say.

- Organise a team building day around Whole Brain Thinking. Assemble a team around you, with which you decide on the topics and activities. Just facilitate, don't spoil it by giving them a tsunami of your ideas.

How Do We All Perceive Each Other?

By now you must have quite an accurate idea of what Whole Brain Thinking can contribute in dealing with VUCA and how it adds to your vertical development. In the previous sections, we have referred to the tables. In this section, we present them to you.

A word of caution is appropriate in this stage. The tables bear no resemblance with the **Ten Commandments**. They are not set in stone. We just give you some examples of how people with different thinking preferences **could** think about other people, having different thinking preferences. By no means are they meant to be used to label other people. Use your senses to find out how the other person prefers to think and that's never exclusively in just one quadrant. Remember that it's always a mix of thinking preferences.

Implement Whole Brain Thinking

Let's do an exercise involving two real persons with dominant thinking preferences in different quadrants.

Think of the relationships you have with these persons.

- Who do you have in mind?
- In which quadrant(s) do you believe that these persons have their dominant thinking preferences?
- Why do you believe that these persons have these quadrants as their thinking preferences? What are your clues?
- What is your relationship with these persons?
- What are, in your view, their strengths and limitations?
- How might your own thinking preferences influence your point of view?
- Which steps can you take to (further) develop your relationship with them?
- Which strengths of them can compensate your blanks?
- Which of your strengths benefits the other person?

Done? Discuss your findings with the persons you have assessed. Don't be afraid to take this step, even if one of them is your manager. Find a common language and have a talk. How can the other person benefit from the Whole Brain Thinking approach?

The Finishing Touch

We've now come to the end of Part 2, describing the NBI™ thinking preferences. This last chapter wrapped it all together in order to reveal the power of Whole Brain Thinking.

You can continue reading the next part(s), but we urge you to take a considerable amount of time to get yourself well acquainted with Whole Brain Thinking. The best way to reach that is to actually do the exercises, preferably together with other people in your team.

One of the best ways to support you in your development is to keep a diary while doing the exercises.

To discover your true thinking preferences, you could do the NBI-adult and leadership profile on our website, www.wholebrainleader.com.

We are fully aware that we occasionally repeated ourselves in this part. Just like we've mentioned in the beginning of the book; this is intentional for the benefit of your learning process.

- ▶ What are your most important insights into Whole Brain Thinking?
- ▶ Which insights can you use, starting today?
- ▶ Which 'dislikes'—from the tables—do you recognise in the people you lead, and how have they influenced your perception about them?
- ▶ In which quadrant would you like to improve your skills? How will you realise that?

Part 3
Lead as a Coach

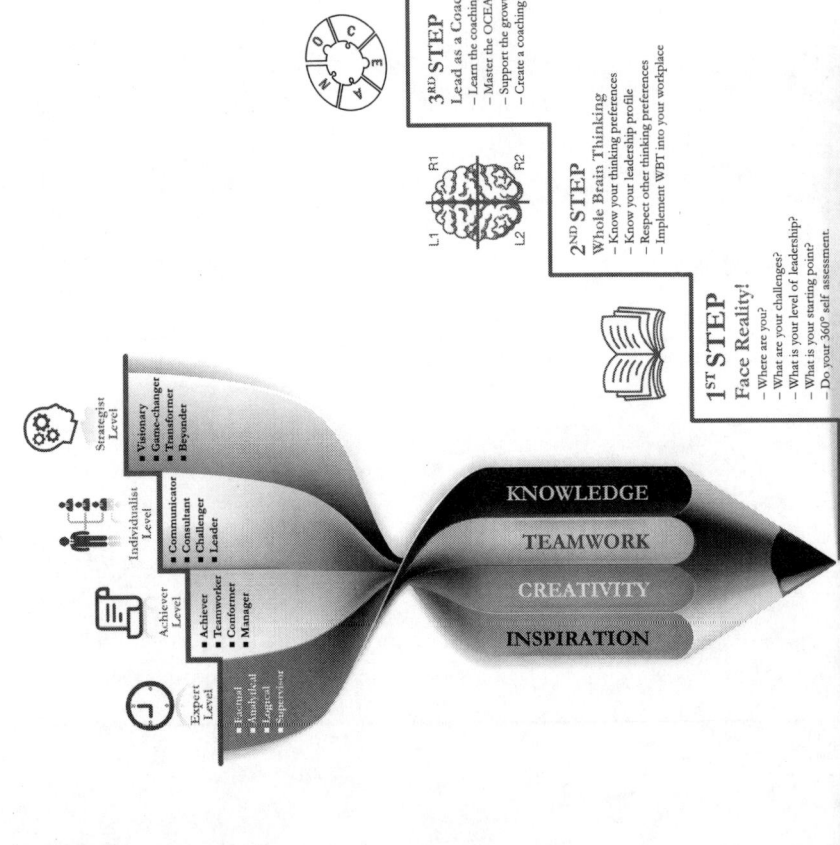

Chapter 9 - A Different Mindset

Now you're entering the next step on your journey towards Whole Brain Leadership. So far, we have mainly worked on your horizontal development. We have shown you the challenges of the modern world in Chapter 1. You have faced reality in Chapter 2, and with the NBI™, you started your journey.

You have seen that Whole Brain Thinking is a powerful mindset in dealing with the challenges and reality as laid out in Part 1 of the book.

We now want to take your Whole Brain Thinking a step further. It would be a shame if you only kept your learning to yourself. In this part of the book, we will discuss how to coach the ones you lead. This way you will not only deepen your own learning, but you will also develop the ones around you as well, resulting in highly collaborative teams.

Make clear decisions on how you will deal with them. It may well be that your roads will split. They might be on a different journey, maybe even on a journey towards the exit of your organisation. So be it, but be clear about it. The world around us is continuously changing, so clarity and commitment on the way forward are essential.

In this chapter, we will also make the connection between Whole Brain Thinking and the leader as a coach. In order to make your coaching successful, we find it necessary to discuss the following subjects:

- The Whole Brain Leader
- Emotional intelligence
- The ego
- The devil on your shoulder
- Desire for improvement

The Whole Brain Leader

What did you learn from the last part? Which insights have you gathered from the exercises? Did it expand your thinking?

Remember, this book is not just meant for reading, you need to practise what you read. Our objective is to help you to effectively deal with VUCA, with all of its challenges. For that, your own mindset is not the only one that needs expansion, but also the minds of the ones you lead. With 'the ones you lead', we go beyond the usual, limited definition of leading. You lead in all directions—up, down and sideways!

Train your brain like you would train the other muscles in your body. Only regular exercising and training will grow your mindset. Reflect and search for answers that will help you grow. Ask others to help you find your answers and offer help to find theirs.

How do you lead now, and how do you want to develop your leadership? Are you already operating at the achiever's level and want to promote yourself towards the individualist stage? Then, start coaching! One of the biggest steps towards that level of leadership is to work on your right-brain skills. Move your focus from the 'how and what' towards the 'who and why'. Use your knowledge of—and capabilities in—Whole Brain Thinking.

Challenge yourself by mixing and matching your Whole Brain Thinking with other leadership concepts, like for instance, situational leadership, principle centred leadership and/or servant leadership.

Emotional Intelligence

In the old days, when everything was nicely organised and much easier to comprehend, we only had to deal with one type of intelligence, the logical type, expressed in IQ. People with a higher IQ had higher education, went to universities and became leaders.

Unfortunately, at a certain stage in the last century, there were scientists who introduced other kinds of intelligence as well. Howard Gardner (1983) published *Frames of Mind: The Theory of Multiple Intelligences*. Suddenly, there were seven different types of intelligence.

In leadership, we believe that both IQ (logical intelligence) and EQ (emotional intelligence) are essential to function well. It wasn't until 1995 that EQ became popular. It was Daniel Goleman (1995) that brought emotional intelligence to the masses. He was inspired by the concept of emotional intelligence in a scientific article, published by Salovey and Mayer (1989).

It wasn't until 2000 that the distinction between the **trait** emotional intelligence and **ability** emotional intelligence was introduced (Petrides and Furnham). We have observed that people with a high emotional intelligence show exemplary job performance and have more potent leadership skills.

There is an issue to keep in mind when discussing EQ. It's very hard to measure, maybe even impossible. IQ tests already have a challenged reputation, and for EQ tests, this is even worse. Exact values are dubious, and that may be a problem for the logical L1 and L2 thinkers amongst us. However, with a 360° assessment, you will get valuable insights into your emotional intelligence.

What exactly is emotional intelligence? It's a mix of traits and the ability to understand and manage your emotions and those of the people around you. When you have high emotional intelligence, you understand your feelings, emotions and how they affect others.

Daniel Goleman (1995) defined five main elements: self-awareness, self-regulation, motivation, empathy and social skills. Let's have a look at what these elements mean for leadership.

1. **Self-awareness**

    If you have high self-awareness, you know your strengths and weaknesses. You know how you feel and why you feel that way. You know how your emotions affect others.

    - What do you think? Would Whole Brain Thinking increase your EQ in this element?

2. **Self-regulation**

    Self-regulation is about maintaining control over your emotions. You know how to avoid overreaction. You don't need to compromise your values when you are strong in self-regulation. Leaders exhibiting self-regulation commit strongly to personal accountability.

    - Would your comprehension of how differently people prefer to think help you in regulating your emotions?

3. **Motivation**

    Strong leaders are intrinsically motivated to work towards their goals. They have very high standards for the quality of their work.

    - Would doing the work you like, in line with your thinking preferences, benefit your motivation?

4. **Empathy**

    Having empathy means that you are able to walk in someone else's shoes. When you have passed the expert level in your leadership development, you have already experienced how critical this element is to the success of the team and organisation. Empathic leaders help the members of their team to develop their skills, give constructive feedback and are deep listeners.

Leaders with a high thinking preference in the R2 dimension empathiser have an advantage. In Chapter 8, we gave you some suggestions on how to train yourself in the R2 quadrant. If you want to further develop your empathy, try some of the exercises mentioned there.

5. **Social skills**

    Leaders with great social skills are also great communicators. They do well in managing change and conflict, and in getting their team's support. R2 leaders with a high preference in the socialiser dimension definitely have an advantage.

Again, we suggest that you look back in Chapter 8 and try some of the exercises mentioned there.

The further you grow in leadership, the more you realise the prominent role emotional intelligence plays. By working on your emotional intelligence, you expand your mindset.

Are we now in an era of leadership where emotional intelligence trumps IQ? We believe that both are (equally) important, but that it may differ from industry to industry, and from organisation to organisation. Fact is that until the end of the last century, the influence of emotional intelligence in effective leadership has been dramatically underestimated.

We have all witnessed highly intelligent leaders fail miserably. They don't know how to get people excited about their ideas and directions. They put huge emphasis on the left brain but don't engage the right brain to support it. This feeds the resistance to change. They are low on emotional intelligence, and, probably, they don't even realise it.

Now that we acknowledge how important emotional intelligence is to the success of the organisation, we should find ways to build on it—not only for ourselves but also for the whole organisation. Leadership should be omnipresent in the organisation, so should be high emotional intelligence.

We can accomplish this by coaching the ones we lead. That is your entry into the vertical leadership development.

The Ego

What do you really know about your ego?

Such a small word, so many (mis)interpretations!

The way Sigmund Freud (1923) defined ego is slightly different from how it is used nowadays. In his structural model of the psyche, he distinguished the Id, the ego and the super-ego (the Id, I and super-I).

The Id is the set of uncoordinated instinctual drives. It wants immediate gratification and seeks to avoid pain and 'unpleasure'. The Id is unconscious and has no judgements about values like good and evil. It's the component of the personality that is present right from birth.

The super-ego is the one constantly watching you for misbehaviour. It can make you feel guilty, anxious and inferior. It sets boundaries around you; it wants you to act responsibly in a socially appropriate manner. You have to follow the rules. The super-ego can seriously restrict your development.

The ego mediates between the Id, the super-ego and reality. The Id and super-ego are the opposites of each other. The ego is the organised component of our personality; it performs reality checks, takes different perspectives, is aware and takes care that the individual functions in the real world. The ego represents reason and common sense.

When you have read the above, doesn't it make you wonder why the ego has received such a bad reputation? Let's be frank. We all have an ego, but maybe for some people, the ego has gone out of control. The way the ego is perceived nowadays is also different from the research conducted by Dr Freud. For the purpose of this book, we will describe the ego as a person's sense of self-esteem or self-worth.

Most of the time, the ego is considered something negative. It is seen as your unrealistic self-image, not your true self. A healthy and positive ego makes you feel good about yourself. The feeling of being enough, not shaken by other people's opinions. You feel balanced and ready to take the next steps in your development. People with a healthy ego also help others to grow. Unfortunately, in these cases, the presence of the ego is taken for granted; there are no signs of appreciation for its good work.

Unhealthy egos get more attention. We consider the inflated and deflated ego as unhealthy examples. When you have an inflated ego, you think too much of yourself. Your self-image is unrealistic and often determined by how you compare to others. Size matters! Do the size of your car, office and your paycheck make you feel more important than others? What about the looks of your spouse or the label on your jacket? Then you probably have an inflated ego, and that will certainly backfire on you when you want commitment from the people you lead.

You can also have the other unhealthy kind—the deflated ego. Then you underestimate your abilities to be successful and want to become invisible. Your ego tells you that you're not good enough. It discourages you from taking risks and keeps you covered. If you let that happen, you'll become insignificant. Initiatives are not the trademark of people with deflated egos.

Did you know that one-on-one conversations usually consist of a group of 4?

When you're coaching as a leader, you will regularly meet both types of unhealthy egos. It may be necessary that you point out that their ego is blocking their development. When you can make them aware that it is a false reflection of the real person, you can help them to construct a more realistic image. Give them the opportunity to adjust their ego to the reality.

As a leader, you have to let go of your own ego as much as you can. Start thinking in terms of 'you and me' instead of 'me'. You should always take the responsibility for your own development as well as the development of your team and organisation. You could use your emotional intelligence to make good connections and recognise when the egos get in the way of development.

In the following chapters, you will learn the basics of coaching as a leader—how to lead your coachee out of his comfort zone and into his development zone. The ego wants to stay in its comfort zone and doesn't appreciate change for what it's worth. You, as a coach, know that real development takes place beyond the boundaries of the comfort zone.

The Devil on Your Shoulder

Are you willing to go the extra mile?

Did you know that one-on-one conversations usually consist of a group of 4? Or should we say 6 or maybe even more? For both participants in the dialogue, there is at least one angel and one devil on their shoulders, both fighting for their attention. We all have multiple selves, and the higher your emotional intelligence, the better you can recognise the different types and deal with them.

This is also part of your vertical leadership development. The higher the level you reach, the better you understand this phenomenon and the more effectively you can employ these different selves in your daily activities, without compromising your values.

In the coaching arena, you will often encounter a range of devilish attitudes, which may undermine both your efforts to coach effectively and your coachee's willingness to be coached, such as cynicism, negativism, unworthiness, escapism, procrastination, to name a few.

Cynicism

Cynicism is an attitude of distrust. A cynic points out why an idea, plan or choice is no good and won't work. He will find flaws in everything and likes to blow them up to huge proportions, overshadowing everything else. Cynicism may come to the surface in the form of a discussion, but it may as well hide itself below the surface, the comments will be left unspoken.

If you see cynicism at play, either with you or your coachee, restore the faith in the ability to improve. Thank the devil for his cynic comments and tell him politely to vanish into thin air. Affirm to yourself or your coachee that far more can be accomplished than the devil is trying to make you believe. Take concrete examples of accomplishments from the past, to reinforce the faith, and project that on the situation at hand.

Negativism

If someone has a tendency to be unconstructively critical towards himself and others, his brain will search for reasons to support this negative attitude. Whatever you (or the devil on your shoulder) tell yourself, your subconscious believes.

With emotional intelligence, this attitude can easily be corrected. First, you have to recognise the negative talk, and then bend it into the positive counterpart. For each situation, there is always a reverse of the medal. Choose the positive side for a change. Whatever you choose, your subconscious believes. You will either trick it with negative thoughts or with the positive counterpart. What will be your choice?

Unworthiness

When someone doesn't believe in positive outcomes, you can call it a deflated ego. The person uses excuses like 'I'm not smart enough', 'I'm too old for this', 'This material is not going to help me', 'I'm too young', 'I'm too inexperienced' and so on. These are clear signs of low self-esteem.

Wake up! Why should you hide yourself? It's that little devil talking to you again, making you feel unworthy and trying to make you as small as he is. Don't feed it with your thoughts. Don't let anyone shrink you verbally. Fix the leak in your ego and give it air. Believe in your capabilities and dare to make mistakes. As a coach, you can create miracles by giving the coachee examples of his successes.

Escapism

The devil on your shoulder may try to lure you away from your path to success. Especially when you find yourself confronted with a bigger challenge, one that will make you feel uncomfortable. Your fight, flight or freeze mechanism cuts in, and you're open to suggestions. The devil on your shoulder is more than happy to share his opinion. He will try to lead you back into your comfort zone, doing things that are far more pleasant. Unfortunately, these activities will not contribute to your development.

Remember that your development takes place outside of your comfort zone. Reflect on situations where the initial feeling of discomfort resulted in successful development. Most people have experienced hard times in their lives. What were hard times for you, and which positive outcomes from these times can you think of after you've left them behind? When your goals are big enough, your problems will shrink in comparison!

Procrastination

This is quite popular among the masses. Have you ever wasted time with trivial activities just to avoid working on what makes a difference? It's the devil on your shoulder again, seducing you to do the pleasant things and put those daunting tasks aside. Instant gratification is within reach, so why should one bother with the long term. Live now and live happily, no matter what the consequences will be for the future.

It's incredibly tempting, and the devil is very convincing. Unfortunately, in time you will experience the consequences of the missed opportunities or the rapidly approaching deadlines. Ask yourself regularly, 'Is this activity I'm involved in now the most important that I can do? Will it bring me closer to fulfilling my big dreams, or is it just a waste of valuable time?'

Don't let the devil on your shoulder beat you in your efforts to grow. Show your strengths and realise your dreams!

A Desire for Improvement

Just the fact that you are reading this book leads us to the assumption that you are highly engaged in your work as a leader and that you are willing to go the extra mile to guide your team and organisation through the VUCA world. We also believe that you will do the exercises in the book and want to start coaching as a leader. We've already mentioned some obstructions you will encounter on your journey, and we have one more for you. One of the challenges you will almost certainly run into is the engagement of your co-workers.

A well-known company, called Gallup, conducts research on employee engagement worldwide. In its latest report, *State of the Global Workplace*,[1] they conclude that worldwide only 13% of the employees are really engaged in their work.

Without going into the details—which, by the way, you should do—you can imagine that your coaching may receive its share of scepticism. A large part of your workforce may not be as engaged as you have anticipated. Your first assignment in your coaching may well be to get them engaged again.

In coaching, it's not about you; it's about the ones you coach. What is keeping them busy? Why is that the case? How engaged are they really? Are they telling you the truth or just what you want to hear? Do they choose socially acceptable answers to your questions? How far will you have to dig to find the true answers? How many layers do you have to peel off before you get to the heart of the matter?

It will be your challenge to increase the engagement. You have to be the example. That will put an extra weight on your shoulders, but it's also part of your own vertical leadership development. You hold the key to Whole Brain Leadership and coaching is probably one of the best ways to improve the level of engagement within the organisation.

In the following chapters, we will provide you with the tools to continue on your journey towards Whole Brain Leadership. **Happy coaching!**

---

[1] See www.gallup.com

- What does your 360° assessment tell you about your ego?
- Which limiting behaviours, as discussed in this chapter, have you experienced yourself?
- Which corrective actions have you taken when it happened?
- How well have you developed your emotional intelligence?
- What are the indications that you are on that level?
- Do you need to improve even further?
- What are your plans?

Chapter 10 – Integrate Coaching into Your Leadership

An increasing number of organisations recognise the value in building a coaching culture. Such a culture offers employees at all levels the opportunity to grow their skills, enhance their value and reach their professional goals.

The organisational benefits from coaching leaders are numerous. Improving the process and speed of decision-making, creating space and time for leaders to focus on other value-adding activities and, most importantly, increasing job satisfaction in general. From the leader's perspective, coaching can both be used as an effective tool and simply as a leadership style.

The different coaching competencies you will learn in the upcoming chapters will inevitably change the way you communicate, not only in the workplace, but in life in general. The coaching process consists of competencies that can be used separately or as a process. You don't have to designate 'coaching-sessions' for your employees to profit from your coaching skills.

Your primary goal of becoming a coaching leader, should be to help people grow, and encourage them to solve problems for themselves, instead of referring them back to you. How would that feel, to have a little more time on your hands, fewer interruptions, and a more independent team?

What Is Coaching?

Is coaching only for professional coaches?

A brilliant definition of coaching comes from Sir John Whitmore (2009), one of the pioneers of coaching and leadership development, and the inventor of the GROW coaching model: 'Coaching is about unlocking people's potential to maximise their own performance. It is helping them to learn rather than teaching them'.

You can use coaching wherever, whenever and with whomever. It is a solution-oriented conversation, or chain of conversations, usually between two individuals. It can also be used for a group of people. It's about helping another person to create the future he desires. It's also about pushing one out of his comfort zone, enhance his motivation and develop his mental strength and willpower. Make him realise, through a series of tough questions, that his growth and fulfilment are always within his reach.

To simplify it even further, coaching is about you having the courage to ask powerful and provoking questions, and keeping your mouth shut when listening.

In relation to other leadership techniques, the value of coaching lies in the empowerment of the ownership. The leader can, through a coaching conversation, create the space for his employee to come up with his own solutions. The employee will go the extra mile to prove himself right and follow through on his solutions.

Coaching in relation to other leadership techniques:

Instruction	Advising	Guidance	Coaching
Clear order	Good advice	A framework to act within	Powerful questions

(Continued)

Instruction	Advising	Guidance	Coaching
The leader only gives content	The leader gives a lot of content, little process	The leader gives little content, much more process	The leader doesn't give content. It's only process
The employee has no ownership in the solution	The employee has little ownership in the solution	The employee has great ownership in the solution	The employee has full ownership in the solution

One of our respected clients, a marketing manager at a private business school, hired a new salesman to reach out to the corporate market—a market they had not actively serviced before. He decided to use the coaching technique whenever he got the opportunity. Each time the salesman approached him with a challenge, he deliberately took him through the process of finding his own solution by asking powerful questions. He not only gave him the chance of viewing his challenges from different perspectives but also the space to reflect on different outcomes. Usually, the freedom to choose the outcome led to the most suitable solution for the challenge he brought in.

Due to his experience, the manager often had all the answers ready, but instead of giving them away, he deliberately created a learning process for the salesman. Often it is tempting to give away the answers instead of going through the process of coaching, but the long-term effects of coaching are unquestionably more beneficial for all parties involved.

In only a few weeks, the new salesman learned that taking shortcuts through his manager was not an option. He learned to practise solution-based thinking, and, even more important, he learned that the manager trusted him to solve his own problems. So instead of showing up with his challenges, he came to the manager to discuss possibilities and options.

The manager afterwards admitted that some of the solutions were far better, and more effective, than the ones he would have suggested. A lesson he would have missed if he had given the answer away in the first place.

The moral of the story? By investing in coaching now, you'll gain much more time and freedom in the long run. You also create a culture of trust and solution-based thinking, which will obviously harvest the best in everyone.

Boss Versus Coach

Are you sure you have all the answers? Then you'd better start asking better questions!

The difference between a boss and a coach is huge. One of the best ways to put it is, 'The boss has all the answers, while the coach has all the questions'. The boss is frequently preoccupied with 'what should be' while driving his team towards his view of the future. The coach starts with the reality, and, with his team, creates a collective vision of 'what could be'.

There is a reason that the head of a baseball team is called the manager and that of a soccer team is called the coach. The manager of a baseball team makes strategies and manages the flow of the game, whereas the coach of a soccer team offers support and ideas on how to react to many possible outcomes. The players of a soccer team are free to implement different plays, using their insights and understanding of the game, depending on the opponent's reaction in the heat of the moment. When the team has a shared vision of the desired results, you should provide them the freedom to achieve them.

Reality is not quite that black and white. There are situations where you have to be directive and to the point. You have to manage your team through times where the pressure of the moment doesn't allow trial and error.

Phil Goodfellow, a manager in a manufacturing plant, had been coaching his team, a knowledgeable group of managers, for years when a fire destroyed a critical part of the factory:

> I immediately had to switch into the manager mode, in order to get the plant back into operation within seven days. I created the need for 'all hands on deck', and a tight coordination of inside staff and emergency repair services. Once we were back up in full production, I went back to coaching mode again.

Increase the Capacity of Others

If you want to become more successful and respected as a leader, you should seriously consider integrating coaching into your leadership no later than now! Becoming a coaching leader is really about expanding your mindset. Take a vertical development step and become more agile to meet tomorrow's challenges. You will see an immediate improvement in performance and development.

A coaching leader creates a Whole Brain culture. Every time you face a challenge, use the four key questions to address all quadrants of the brain:

- Do we have all the facts (L1)?
- Do we have a plan to follow (L2)?
- Do we have everybody we need on board (R2)?
- Are there alternative solutions (R1)?

A coaching leader also builds bridges between the generations. He connects the experience of the baby boomers with the technical savvy of Generation Y, or better, he lets them find out for themselves.

Many organisations have trouble attracting and retaining Generation Y employees. Great coaches listen and let them discover and share what keeps them motivated. It makes retaining generation Y easier. In fact, it makes retaining every generation easier.

Some baby boomers feel that they have trouble keeping pace. Again, great coaches let them express their feelings and rethink their roles. At the core, everyone wants to contribute and leave a legacy. Small changes may get derailed baby boomers back on track. Who wins?

How can a great coach help members of Generation X the forgotten generation? How about listening to their unique stories? Their careers have, more than with the other generations, scars from difficult times. If they were able to survive, they can be valuable advisors.

Imagine the strength and the flexibility you could create. Employees can't move forward if they don't leave their comfort zones.

From Two-way to Three-way Communication

From conversation to coaching: open up the third way.

A conversation is usually a form of interactive, natural dialogue between two or more people. There is a conversation holder and at least one other participant with whom the subject is familiar. That is called a symmetric relation. When the leader takes the role as a coach and uses powerful questions, he creates space for the third voice in the conversation, the silent inner voice of his employee.

Instead of listing up ideas and options, he asks questions: 'What do you see as the best possible outcome?' or David Allen's (2001) favourite question in his Getting Things Done-system: 'What does DONE look like to you?'

This is a three-way conversation where the coach challenges his coachee, creates awareness and polarised thinking where he juggles with different perspectives. It results in creative and critical thinking. It leaves the employee with the heightened awareness and ownership of whatever solution comes out of the conversation.

Bringing Coaching into Your Workplace

Your workplace culture is the sum of the collective behaviour of the people in your organisation. It's the grand total of all member's ethics, values, beliefs, objectives and ambitions. It's also a blend of what the different generations and people with different thinking preferences bring to the table. Influencing and changing some of these factors, to drive new behaviours, takes time. If you read and apply the next chapters, where we teach you the basic skills of coaching, we can guarantee that investing the time and effort in integrating coaching into your workplace will pay off, both in the short and the long runs.

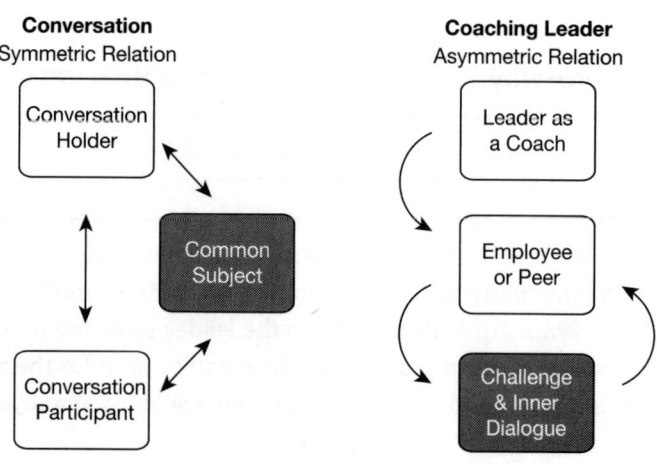

A coaching leader encourages people to think and act for themselves and take responsibility for their actions. Unfortunately, there will always be someone who avoids responsibility at any cost. Some just want to be told what to do, when and how to do it. However, since the need for growth is one of our basic needs, you might consider using your coaching skills to find out what is really holding him back.

Creating a coaching culture is—all at the same time—challenging, encouraging and exciting! A corporate coaching culture encourages people to speak up and express their opinions, even if they differ from the rest. It reduces the fear of failure because people are taught to treat mistakes and setbacks as treasured learning experiences. Therefore, people become more willing to take risks and contribute their ideas, resulting in a variety of new opportunities. Everybody benefits. It amplifies meaningful communication and encourages people to give constructive and motivating feedback. A coaching culture in the workplace builds confidence, allows teams to grow stronger, improves performance and increases productivity.

When Is Coaching Appropriate?

Coaching should not be bound to a specific time or place. Sometimes you create a situation where you lead someone through an organised coaching session (you don't have to call it that; just call it a meeting) with a specific task at hand. Sometimes, you are just amplifying and motivating people on the run. There are no rights or wrongs as long as the intention is right. Coaching often sounds formal, but most of the time, it shouldn't be.

Everybody has the potential to be(come) a coaching leader. A coaching leader is more about being than doing. As a coaching leader, you are constantly looking for growth opportunities in the people around you. Asking powerful questions will become natural to you. You will automatically start elevating your own awareness to higher levels, you learn to listen in greater depths and people will start to notice that just being around you creates energy and buoyancy.

OCEAN: Our Model for Coaching

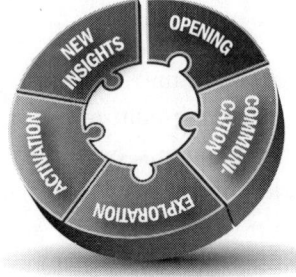

When you learn a new game, it helps to know and understand the rules. There are not many rules in coaching, but there is a simple framework that we have created. We have called it the OCEAN model and successfully use it in our work as coaches. It is simple, strategic and easy to follow, has a clear beginning, middle and an end. It helps to keep the dialogue flowing and concise.

- Opening
- Communication
- Exploration
- Activation
- New insights

O—Opening

Sometimes you have a specific subject you want to address with an employee; sometimes it's the employee who owns an issue he wants to discuss. In all cases, regardless of who owns the topic, it's very important to start on the right foot.

Create the right environment for your coaching session.

In the opening phase, the most important thing is to create a safe and positive environment where people can open up. That is the indispensable groundwork for the rest of the conversation. If you fail to create the right environment, or if there is tension or scepticism in the air, the results of the coaching session will never be a true success. Professional coaches use this phase to discuss confidentiality and trust. We encourage you to invest the time necessary to create an atmosphere that supports a motivating and value-adding conversation with your coachee.

In the beginning of a coaching session, it is vital to reach a mutual agreement regarding the topic of the conversation. Ask questions like: 'Do we agree that we use this time to focus on this particular topic?' or 'What is the most important issue we need to address here and now?' Agreeing on the matter makes it easier for you to keep the rest of the conversation on track. You hold the reins, and you should prevent the conversation from jumping from one subject to another. How often have you started discussing topic **A** and before you knew the meeting was over, you have discussed the surface of **B**, **C** and **D** without any conclusions at all on **A**.

A mutual understanding of the main purpose of the conversation makes it easier for you to maintain your direction and move the conversation back on track whenever an irrelevant issue enters the conversation.

C—Communication

We all have different ways of communicating with each other. We might share the same language, but factors such as background, gender, race, generations and values often result in a gap in understanding. The common understanding is, therefore, far too often some form of misunderstanding.

Effective and conscious communication is essential. It avoids unnecessary assumptions and helps you to stay on the same page.

E—Exploration

Have you got the courage to dive in deep?

The exploration phase is the heart of every coaching conversation. This is where it all happens. When the groundwork is ready, you should get down to business. There you start exploring the pros and the cons, options and alternatives, how to build on the past and flirt with the future. You dive in all the way! What is underneath the surface? What drives the other person's behaviour? What are his expectations, values and driving factors?

Look at the conversation as a mental journey. Create a space without boundaries where you explore the best possible outcome and elevate your coachee's awareness.

In the following chapters, you will discover different ways to dig for reality. You will learn how to lead someone beyond the fear of failure. In the exploration phase, your coachee will face obstacles and your main task will be to help overcome them mentally, before planning the way through, around or over them. It is the most challenging phase for you because it demands courage to dive under the surface and maintaining full control over your ego.

A—Activation

Following the exploration phase, you get into 'the recipe mode'. What is the best possible outcome? What is its recipe? What needs to be done? What is the first logical step? Establishing goals, designing actions, creating a plan and breaking it down to smaller goals is the best way to get people to follow through.

However, it's important that you do not enter into the 'Activation' phase too early in the conversation. That is the single most frequent mistake leaders make in their coaching sessions. By rushing to actions and goals, you drive people's minds away from creating awareness, from the 'what, why and who', and push them immediately into the practical 'how and when'.

N—New insights

After a session or conversation, the coachee should have gained new insights, at least around the specific issue that has been discussed. This is the phase in which he collects his thoughts. You give him space to 'try them on' and link his emotions with his intentions. Use the space to provide him with positive feedback on the results of the session and affirm his excitement about his new goals and actions. Affirm his ability to follow through on the plans as agreed upon and ensure him that you will support him, if so needed and requested. Support should then be in the form of further coaching. The coachee should always remain the owner of the change.

▶ What is the first step for you to start implementing coaching into your leadership?

▶ How will coaching serve you as a leader?

▶ What do you already know about coaching?

Chapter 11 - Opening

In this chapter, we discuss the significant role of rapport. You can't choose your relatives, and the same thing is often true when it comes to your co-workers. Therefore, you sometimes have to create circumstances and rapport with people that don't necessarily share your worldview.

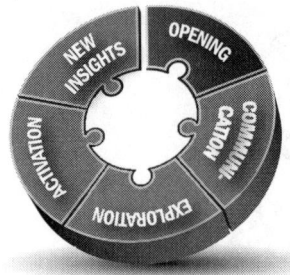

As a leader, you need to master your ability to see the world through their eyes and understand where they are coming from. If you want to influence someone constructively, you need good rapport. Creating rapport is about you being able to create the environment where both parties can be open without a feeling of dominance, power distance or tension. Don't be shy to bring up the issue of honesty and trust: 'What goes on in this room, stays in this room!'

Your Presence

Your presence is greatly determined by how other people feel around you. Your presence has everything to do with how easy or challenging it is for others to create rapport with you. Not only for your co-workers, but in life in general.

If you have a powerful presence, it can surely help you to get what you want. You should use your presence for the greater good rather than for egocentric and selfish goals. It's not a measurement of one's kindness. It's a way of being and can also be the biggest obstacle when it comes to creating rapport.

In your relation with others, what they hear and see when they consort with you, comes down to their perception of your presence. What you say is not what you say; what you say is what they hear. The words you use only form a minor part of what they perceive. Your voice and your body language count for much more.

It's interesting to look at how the different thinking quadrants of the brain are perceived by others. An L1 is sometimes perceived as, brilliant but stiff, deep but distant, calm but confronting. An L2 is seen as inflexible but detailed, square but steadfast. The R1 is often seen as 'all over the place', lacking structured arguments, but also as the genius creator of alternatives, and the R2 as too emotional and resilient, but as the glue that holds the team together.

Are you able to let your coachee discover his limiting beliefs?

Another variable to be aware of is the way generations approach each other. Imagine you're a member of Generation Y, trying to coach a baby boomer. Can you imagine his thoughts about you coaching him? As a coach, you should be able to understand the feelings of your coachee. Another nice example is the other way around, the baby boomer coaching a millennial. As a coach, you'd better be prepared for radically different points of view.

Regardless of your thinking preference, you should adapt to your coachee, especially in the beginning of a coaching conversation. Creating rapport is like dancing. It helps if you are dancing in the tempo of the song. Otherwise, it could feel more like wrestling. People with great presence reflect on people's emotions, attitudes and situations, and then adapt to them.

Relating to People's Potential

One of the core values of the coaching leader is to believe in, and relate to, other people's potentials. There is always more to every individual than meets the eye. Most of the time, people do not comprehend their own true potential. They need someone to help them see what they are truly capable of.

People's behaviour is the manifestation of their values, beliefs and expectations. In a coaching conversation, you often reach the point where your coachee has to face his limiting beliefs and behaviour. Then you need to dive under the surface and explore, together with your coachee, the roots of these limiting beliefs and behaviour. Without good rapport, that could be very challenging for both parties.

The Basics of Rapport

People are generally more receptive to people with whom they share similarities. According to the bestselling book *Social Intelligence* by Daniel Goleman (2006), the most primitive parts of the human brain are connected to the ability to read expressions and actions in order to define whether a person is friend or foe.

We are constantly, consciously and subconsciously reading signals in people's behaviour. These signals—gestures, body language and tone of voice—will help you creating rapport. The easiest way is called matching and mirroring. You have heard the expression 'opposites attract'? Well, it's true for magnets, but it isn't true for people the same way. The significance of mirroring is one of the most powerful ways of creating rapport. It's like being 'in sync' or being on the same wavelength as the person with whom you are talking. You create a sense of 'sameness'. The most obvious forms of mirroring are yawning and smiling. When you see someone yawn, or even if you just read the word 'yawn', you are more than likely to yawn in the next 20 seconds.

Let's stop yawning and take a look at some of the things you could match and mirror to create better rapport.

The Voice

Mirroring the voice is easy. But be careful! You are most likely coaching people who know you, so do not change your normal voice; rather adjust it to the circumstances. Mirroring the voice is about three variables, the tone, tempo and timbre. The tone of the voice refers to its pitch and frequency. The tempo is about speed and rhythm, and the timbre is about the characteristics of the voice. Do not speak faster than the other person; this makes him feel pressured. Try to speak at the same, or slightly slower, pace than the other person.

The biggest challenge to voice mirroring is most likely in your way of listening. To hear what people are truly saying, you have to wrap your awareness around how people use their voice. You can only listen to one conversation at a time. You are either paying attention to the person who is speaking, and how he speaks, or to your own thoughts about what you are going to say next.

To be able to mirror the voice, you must listen carefully. You will be amazed about how your coaching skills will improve at the same time. Your perception of others will be enriched.

Body Language

Mirroring body language is a nonverbal way to say 'I am like you, I feel the same'. When people say that the 'vibes' are right around a particular person, they are likely to be referring to mirroring and synchronous behaviour that they may not even be aware of consciously.

When you mirror body language, you are consciously using your body language to mirror the subconscious actions and gestures of the other person. But it must be done in a way that remains unnoticed at their conscious level. It is important that you do not 'copycat' their movements. Use similar body language or gestures roughly 10 seconds after they have. Never mirror other person's negative body language; you will just feed off negative vibes.

At this stage, you are not really reading the other person's body language; you are simply mirroring it. Don't get surprised however, if you will subconsciously start to comprehend how the other person is feeling. Mirroring generates a deeper understanding and rapport, and it works both ways.

Trust

Building trust is all in your hands! Start by being trustworthy.

In the old leadership model, being a leader was a vertical function, related to power. Today things have changed. The business world has moved away from the vertical structure towards networks. The power-based leadership has lost its relevancy. Leaders who can successfully gain trust from their employees will generate rapport effortlessly.

Trust is a complicated issue to define. Therefore, we use the trust equation. It demonstrates how you can build trust by being a trustworthy coaching leader: $T = (C+R+I+R+P/SI)$. Simple, right? Our trust equation includes six variables to measure trust. Every one of them plays an important role and will damage your trustworthiness if neglected.

The WBL Trust Equation

$$\text{Trust} = \frac{\text{Credibility} + \text{Reliability} + \text{Intimacy} + \text{Relationship} + \text{Positive Intent}}{\text{Self Interest}}$$

Credibility is related to what we say. You should say what you mean, in a way that others can comprehend. You should stay true to your words and stick to the facts when possible.

Reliability has to do with what you do. You walk your talk. A person who is reliable does not leave a gap between what he says and what he does.

Intimacy is to put your head as well as your heart into a situation. It is about respect for the other person and making him feel that you are completely engaged in the conversation.

Relationship is how well you already know the person you are coaching. If your relationship is mature and strong, you might easily create rapport. But if your relationship is weak, or relatively new, you may consider to give all variables above the line a bit more of your time and attention.

Positive intent is the opposite of having a double agenda. It's to get people to trust that the conversation they are about to enter into is about them, their opportunities and their abilities to develop skills or overcome challenges.

Self-interest is the common denominator. You and your ego are irrelevant at this point. Eliminate your self-interest in the conversation. This is a challenge for many leaders, especially those who usually fill up the room.

The Scale of Rapport

It surely helps when you're able to put your finger on something as intangible as rapport. In her book, *Brilliant Coaching*, Julie Starr (2011) introduced the scale of rapport.

Scale of rapport

5	Support, trust, positively connected
4	Strong sense of knowing, the familiar
3	Genuine warmth, kinship
2	Comfortable, familiar
1	Some warmth
0	Neutral
-1	Hesitation, trepidation
-2	Some discomfort, detachment
-3	Awareness of dislike, disassociation
-4	Genuine aversion, antipathy, real dislike
-5	Stronger, hostile feelings, even loathing

Source: Brilliant Coaching by Julie Starr (2011).

> *How easily can you build rapport?*
> *Is that the same with everybody?*

How to Build Rapport?

Now that you have some of the basics, here are some practical steps to get started:

- Create a relaxed atmosphere.
- Smile and use direct eye contact.
- Show an authentic interest in the other person as a human being.
- Be natural; don't try to be someone you are not.
- Use open body language. Keep your arms and legs uncrossed in the beginning.
- Stay away from the computer.
- Face your coachee and lean into the conversation.
- Questions about family or interests may prove to be helpful.
- Pick up on cues from the responses.
- Notice the tone, tempo and timbre of his voice and try to adapt.
- Try to determine where you are on the scale of rapport.
- Notice what might be causing a lack of rapport.
- Mirror your partner and send him the message that you understand what he feels.

Poor rapport is like skating on thin ice. The whole conversation relies on the quality of the rapport you manage to create in the beginning of the conversation.

The Best Possible Outcome

The main reason for good rapport is to be able to get to the bottom of things without using the power of authority. There is a huge difference talking about things as they are and how they could be, instead of how they were and should be.

Our favourite questions to get on the same page and to create collective awareness in the beginning are: 'What is the best possible outcome of our conversation today?' and 'What specific issue do we need to clarify to ensure effective progression in…?'

It cannot be overstated how important it is to reach a common understanding on the purpose at the beginning of the conversation. Remember, the core information for your conversation will be under the surface. You will experience that when the conversation reaches a certain level or a delicate issue comes up for discussion, your coachee will be tempted to change the subject or steer away. That is where the value of 'the agreement' kicks in, to be able to stick to the agreement.

You might, however, find out in the middle of your conversation that what you agreed upon in the beginning is only a by-product of a bigger issue. Then you should embrace this new discovery, reflect on it and 'rewrite' your agreement.

- How is your rapport with your closest co-workers today?
- What could you do to improve the rapport you have with the people working closest to you?
- What is the result of your trust equation?

Chapter 12 – Communication

Nothing in this world has any meaning but the meaning you give it! The true meaning of communication often gets lost in the perception. Communication is more than the exchange of information. It's about perception and understanding the true meaning, the underlying emotions and objectives.

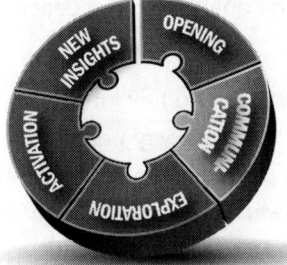

This chapter is about how you can become a better communicator and your ability to convey your message so that it is received exactly the way you intended.

The quality of your communication has four cornerstones:

- the quality of your questions
- your ability to listen to what is really being told
- the way you give feedback
- the courage to be direct in your communication

It often takes courage to get to the bottom of things and communicate directly. It would be so much easier if people could just say what they mean and mean what they say in a way the other can comprehend it. But that is rarely the case.

The Power of Questions

A conversation without questions is like the battle of egos fighting for space.

How to find the right answers?
Simple, just ask the right questions!

There are numerous reasons for asking questions, but the quality of the information we receive depends on the quality of the questions we ask. Smart questions often generate smart answers, the same way as poor questions lead to poor answers. The quality of your questions also determines the quality of your coaching conversation.

Great leaders are generally expert questioners. They know how to ask powerful questions—the ones that shift the way people think. Great questions create awareness that often results in 'out of the box' solutions and success. With powerful questions, you can empower anyone to think outside his box and come up with solutions they didn't know they had within them. We can quote Albert Einstein on that: 'We cannot solve our problems with the same thinking we used when we created them'.

That is the core purpose of questions in a coaching conversation, to release the hidden power and potential of your coachee. With the right questions, you can break down mental barriers. When someone seems to be stuck with a problem, you can ask unconventional questions that might guide him towards unconventional solutions and, most importantly, you can do it without taking away the ownership. People tend to be more motivated to work towards their own solutions. Even though you know the answer, you are offering him the gift of ownership and increase his self-esteem and motivation—all at the same time.

The power of questions is absolute. The one who is asking the question is the one leading the conversation. You should, however, use that power with respect.

Effective Questions

In your situation as a coaching leader, an effective question reveals the information needed to maximise the benefit of the employee. The questions should be both meaningful and understandable. Effective questions generate the space in which an employee is allowed to step back to reflect on himself. They amplify discovery, increase insights, empower commitment and lead to action. They move people forward, closer to their goals. They don't require justification or excuses.

You might (and have the right to) ask questions about what is holding your employee back, but be sure to frame it constructively. 'Why haven't you finished?' is a question that cries out for an excuse. 'What steps do you need to take to complete the task?' is a more constructive way to reach the same goal.

Plan Your Questions

An effective way to get into the right mindset before the coaching session begins is to plan some of your questions, similar to a musician planning his set before going on stage. There are a lot of questions you can't directly prepare for, but you could frame the session/conversation by asking yourself some effective questions:

- What is the best possible outcome for this conversation?
- Which questions would challenge the coachee?
- Which questions could motivate him?

- Which questions would increase his awareness and move him forward?
- Which questions could move him closer to his next level of development?

The answers to those questions will create momentum. They will get you into the right mindset and focused on the core and your main purpose.

How Not to Ask Questions?

There are less effective questions as well. The dos and don'ts.

Vague questions, where the coachee is unsure of what is being asked for, are ineffective. Loaded or leading questions, that point the coachee's answer in a certain direction, are also in a grey area. There are however exceptions to that. Sometimes you may have to use loaded questions to lead the conversation into an area of development. Stay away from 'why' questions. They can feel confrontational and judgmental. You can get to the same point by asking 'What was your intention, when you decided to…?'

When you learn to appreciate the power of good questions, it's easy to get carried away. If you have a number of powerful questions lined up, you might forget the most important part of the process, to listen. Each question you ask gets your coachee into a thinking process. He might not answer your question right away, which is good. Avoid interrupting him with yet another question. This will only interrupt his reflections and confuse him. Stick to one question at the time, and allow your coachee to engage with it. Make his brainpower shine.

Beware of rhetorical questions. They can be natural to ask, but tricky to answer. 'How can we plan ahead if we don't have a plan in the first place?' A question like that is judgmental, not a way forward and doesn't motivate the coachee. 'What do we need to make an effective plan?' or 'What does a good plan look like to you?' are better alternatives, and will undoubtedly move your coachee into the right direction.

Avoid complicated and overloaded questions at any cost. 'Considering, if we want to move forward with this, knowing that our core competencies are not supporting the company to move in this direction and our competitors have not been challenging us in the area, but the market is likely to embrace the new product, what could be the best way forward?' Wouldn't you be confused? It's better to be clear and to the point. 'What do we need to move forward?' is a question that serves the same purpose and clears the way for fresh thinking.

Types of Questions

Closed-ended questions are usually easy to answer, but their effectiveness is limited since they simply require a 'Yes' or 'No' answer, or a specific piece of information. They may be used early in conversations to encourage participation, to identify a certain piece of information or to test the understanding of a particular issue. But closed-ended questions can bring conversations to a squeaking halt. They are often used to confront people, but in most cases the effectiveness of the question increases if you can 'open' it up. Instead of asking 'Is that important to you?', you should ask 'How important is that to you?' and even add 'On a scale from 1 to 10?'

Open-ended questions usually begin with 'who, what, why, where, how or when'. By contrast to closed questions, they allow for longer responses and, therefore, more creativity and information. Open-ended questions should encourage the respondent to think and reflect. But the true value (for you as a coach) is that they reveal his underlying beliefs, opinions, and feelings. Open-ended questions often temporarily transfer the control of the conversation to the respondent. That is also fine, because the coaching session is not about you, remember? As a coach you can always take the wheel back by asking new questions.

Some open-ended questions are closed by nature, like fact seeking questions 'Who participated in the meeting?' If you want to avoid closed-ended questions, you should avoid these verbs in the beginning of a question: haven't, didn't, aren't, would, are, was, will and won't. 'Haven't we discussed that already?' As you see, this question is not a way forward.

Probing questions are used when you want to help your coachee to search for more detail and reflect further on a particular issue or scenario. There are some probes you can use, depending on where the conversation is going to and what you want them to discover:

- What are the pros and cons of the situation?
- What do we already know about this?
- Is there anything we are missing out?
- How does this relate to what we are discussing?
- What exactly did you mean when you said…?
- What would be an example of an outstanding…?
- If this is what we need to continue, what would be the best…?
- What exactly does this mean?
- What is the nature of…?

Principles of Listening

Be silent for a change. You will learn so much more by listening.

Mark Twain once said, 'If we were supposed to talk more than we listen, we would have two tongues and one ear'. Listening is key to all effective communication, but what you hear is too often quite far from what is being told.

Prepare yourself for listening. Let go of your usual assumptions; listen with respect and an open and reflective mind. Focus on their needs and concerns, and put other things 'on hold'. If you catch your mind wandering away from the conversation, you are not present. The coachee will notice that immediately. Concentrate on the coachee, keep eye contact, use 'mirroring-techniques' to open up the coachee, and let him feel at ease.

The first actions you should take, if you want to improve your listening skills, are to stop talking and to tame your ego! When listening, don't interrupt or talk over your coachee. Even when you think you know better, or have an opinion on the matter. Don't steal the conversation away from him.

The next step is to not only listen to what they are saying, but also to how they say it.

You should learn to 'listen between the lines'. Apart from the words he is using, notice if his verbal and nonverbal message are in sync. Is his body language supporting his words? What about his facial expressions. It's crucial to 'listen' to the whole body, because words are only playing a marginal role in the actual conversation.

Sometimes people don't mean what they say, and their body can't hide it. It's easy to control words, but subconsciously the body is harder to control. Someone might tell you that he is happy with the team performance through gritted teeth, or with his arms crossed, both implying the opposite. If that is the case, you should clarify what you saw, and point it out. 'I hear what you say, however there seems to be a mismatch between what you say and how you feel about it' (direct communication).

One of the most powerful tools you can use in your coaching is silence. It can be challenging for your patience, but don't underestimate the power of silence and patience. If your coachee is explaining something, you should bite your tongue before responding too soon. If you stay quiet after he speaks, it will in most cases force him to elaborate a bit further on whatever answer he has already given, and most often on a deeper level than before. Silence is golden when coaching. Be patient and give the coachee the space he needs to reflect on his thoughts and formulate his answers.

Remember the Whole Brain? Seek to understand the other person's point of view. You might be a left-brainer and your coachee a right-brainer. You might prefer the conversation to be organised, structured and based on facts and figures while on the other side your coachee is grabbing bits and pieces from the whole picture, even mixing feelings with facts. Do you see how easy it is to become irritated when the coachee truly needs you to be impartial?

Whatever you do, remember the nature of coaching. It's not about you! It's about your ability to help people grow and learn. Listen with all your senses and you will begin to understand your coachee on a level you haven't heard of before.

Feedback

How can you know if you're doing well, when you don't get feedback?

A 'laissez-faire' management style, where you expect your people to solve problems on their own, can be both practical and constructive. If you feel that your people are failing to reach their full potential, or not recognising areas of improvements, it's your responsibility to step in and give them feedback.

Feedback is an effective way to help others learn more about themselves and the effect their behaviour and performance has on others.

Constructive feedback increases self-awareness, offers guidance and inspires development. Too much negative, critical feedback can harm the morale and productivity, since it leaves employees feeling under-appreciated. Bear in mind that constructive feedback does not mean that you are only giving positive feedback or praise. Critical feedback delivered in the right way, with good intentions, can be just as vital and useful. As a coaching leader, you want people to give feedback to you as much and often as possible. In many cases, however, feedback is not needed at all.

From a generation point of view, be aware that millennials are less concerned with providing feedback to the organisation than Generation X. So, if you want to get their feedback on organisational matters, you specifically have to solicit for it. Generation X members will give it, even if you haven't asked for it.

When you are giving feedback, you should prepare yourself and remember it's a process. When you offer feedback, you might want to consider beginning your feedback with a positive. Any following negative is then more likely to be heard. It's similar to the opening of our OCEAN-coaching model. If, however, your relation with the coachee is mature and strong, you shouldn't spend time wrapping your feedback in cotton. Just raise your concerns and get to the point!

Be concrete and clear about what you mean. 'You did an excellent job in the meeting' is far too general and vague. Pinpoint specifically what made you use the word excellent. 'The way you framed your arguments in the meeting, totally convinced them—excellent job!' is a much more effective and reinforcing way to give feedback. If someone is talking about the commitment of the team, grab the opportunity (at the right moment and if it adds value to the conversation) to give positive feedback, 'I can hear how important the commitment of the team is to you', and then use the power of silence to give him the space to elaborate on that. What will follow, is likely to be one level deeper, attached with feelings and reasons for the importance of the team. But what you are implying with this intervention is 'I am truly listening'.

Focus on the situation—not the person and on the behaviour—not the personality. 'YOU gave a bad presentation today; YOU left people hanging' is an example of attacking the person. 'The presentation you gave today didn't meet our standards—it left people with more questions than answers' is a better way. The best way, of course, is to start with the positives and be specific about the areas of development. 'I liked the way you responded to all the questions after your presentation, AND (don't use the word BUT) I'm sure you can use many of these questions to improve your next week's presentation, to get an even sharper focus, what do you think?'

A coaching leader, however, should give the person the benefit of the doubt. There is a fat chance the presenter is fully aware of how bad his presentation was. Then he doesn't need that kind of feedback. What he needs is a little coaching. He needs space to reflect on his performance. 'I noticed you got an unusual amount of questions after your presentation today!' Then just give him the gift of silence. If he gets defensive, you could try a scaling question. 'On the scale from five to ten, how do you think your presentation went?' Starting at five implicates that you are not 'failing' him. He might respond with a seven. Then, in his mind, he is admitting a 30% room for improvement. What a great start of a coaching conversation. 'What would this presentation have looked like if you would have delivered it at a nine?' Do you spot the difference?

Direct Communication

Direct communication gives clarity, but it doesn't always feel comfortable.

Have you ever heard someone saying 'I like him because I know exactly where I have him'? You have probably also been left hanging after a conversation. Not knowing how to act or react to the message. Was there a message? You heard the words, but you had the unpleasant feeling that the truth was left untold. That is the difference between direct and vague communication. What would you prefer?

As a coaching leader, you should invest your time and awareness in mastering the way you communicate. You should set a positive example, communicate clearly and ensure that your words have the same meaning as you are conveying through your posture, gestures, facial expressions and eyes. Imagine someone rolling his eyes saying, 'We really have to focus here!' It doesn't make sense.

Direct communication is often outside people's comfort zone. Let people know that clear and direct communication is valued. Help them to get to the point, to the core of things. That is where the true value lies.

You can use the whole brain to ensure understanding. It helps to use 'the right' language to have the greatest positive impact:

- Let's get all the facts on the table (L1).
- Let's take it step-by-step, so nothing is left out (L2).
- Let's take a look at the whole picture (R1).
- Let's talk, not only face-to-face, but also heart-to-heart (R2).

- Which questions, in your business environment, can you ask to help your coachees reducing their fears for change? Think of several possibilities per quadrant.
- Which challenging questions can you ask your organisation's top management to get their commitment to implement Whole Brain Leadership?
- When will you ask these questions?
- In what way can listening to their objections help you to reduce their fears of change?

Chapter 13 – Exploration

In this chapter, we reach the heart of the coaching conversation, the exploration phase. You can compare the OCEAN coaching model with a fishing trip. Until now, we have only made the preparations.

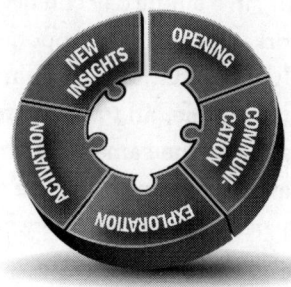

The **Opening,** where you create rapport with your coachee, can be seen as a fishing boat. A good rapport is like a reliable and seaworthy boat, while poor rapport is more like fishing with a leaking wreck. In that case, the focus is too much on the vessel, instead of on the content of the conversation. A leaking hole in the bottom of the boat could be the manifestation of any element above the line in the Trust-equation (p. 127). The ballast of the boat is below the line, your ego. Too much of your ego will sink the boat; too little ego will capsize it.

You can compare the **Communications** part of the model with your fishing gear. The more you develop your communication skills, the better is your chance of 'catching' something of value. The only thing you should bear in mind is; you may well be the captain of the conversation, but the coachee should be the one taking the catch home. The coaching conversation is always about generating awareness and the coachee's learning process. You should not use it as a power-tool nor to satisfy your own curiosity.

As a coaching leader, you can transform the culture of your organisation one mindset at the time. The VUCA storm might create waves on the surface, for example, irritation and pin pricking behaviour. The world in which we lead is like the ocean, the only thing we see is above the surface and represented by effects. It's below the surface, that you will find the causes of these effects. If you lack the leadership courage to dive in, and only work with what you see, you will not be able to increase the coachee's self-awareness and tap into his highest aspirations and talents.

Cognitive Dissonance

In the theatre of life, we play numerous roles. The roles we might be playing in a single day can be: the father/mother, friend, teammate, co-worker, boss, lover, opponent and soul mate, to name a few. In a VUCA world, those roles are often in conflict. Every role needs attention, time, and mental resources. People crave balance and oversight at the same time, and therefore they find it challenging to manage their roles and the sometimes conflicting interests. That often generates a gap between people's intentions and actions, called cognitive dissonance. Conflicting beliefs and actions can quickly cause inner conflict and stress.

Are you aware of all the roles you play?

We hold many cognitions about the world and ourselves; when they clash, a discrepancy is evoked, resulting in a state of tension (Festinger 1957). In live, some primary factors drive our actions. We want to avoid pain and gain pleasure. Most of us desire cognitive consistency. The coaching leader really should have that notion as one of his guiding lights in his coaching conversations.

What Is the Actual Reality?

As you probably know by now, coaching is about fishing for reality, finding the facts and the truth in the situation, to create cognitive consistency. Coaching is not about the symptoms; it's going to deeper water and fish for the causes. It's about exploring what drives people's behaviour, and to help them understand that the solutions are almost always within themselves. There are more solutions than problems in the world and coaching is about finding, evaluating, and acting on the best solutions applicable to the situation.

To be able to think clearly in a VUCA environment, it's critical to take regular reality checks. In a coaching conversation, you lead your coachee through the powerful process of facing reality, thinking, reflecting, deciding, planning and doing. Just remember how important it is to focus and reflect on what is—before you start wondering about what could, would and should be.

Self-respect Leads to Self-confidence

When there is a gap between what people say and do, it inevitably affects their self-confidence. In our seminars, we often ask the question 'what is self-confidence?' The answers we get are mostly quite 'far-off'. People tend to over-complicate the issue. Your self-confidence is the manifestation of your self-respect. Period!

Have you ever broken the little promises you made to yourself? Haven't we all? Would you like to live together with a person who breaks as many promises to you, as you do to yourself?

When we ask our customers this particular question, they tend to put up a funny face, grin or laugh. But we have to face the reality, and the reality is, in the big picture, that people often have difficulties realising the long-term consequences of their short-term actions.

Every time they fail to follow up on their words with corresponding actions, they are cognitively inconsistent. Habitually they are too focused on short-term victories, lacking the vision to follow up on their long-term goals (assuming they have these in the first place).

People can develop and strengthen their self-confidence through self-respect, in the same way, a tree gets its lifeblood through its roots. Self-respect is therefore nothing more and nothing less than people's trust in their ability to deliver on what they promise themselves.

Many of our customers get an epiphany when they see this metaphor. It's so obvious and so easy to comprehend. We all want to break the negative patterns in our lives, do more of the rational things we know are good for us, and less of what we know that is holding us back. Delivering to yourself is the perfect starting point.

The reason we bring this up here is that you will find yourself in this situation numerous times. When you start fishing for the reality, people will start to admit that they know far too well what needs to be done, they have the answers but they haven't (yet) found the emotional leverage to follow through. There you should use the metaphor about the self-respect to get them to realise the long-term value of determination.

The Gift of Reflection

Paying attention to our cognitive inconsistency is not something we usually do on a daily basis. We don't allow ourselves the time or space to focus on what matters most. We know that you have heard this before, but there is another reason for bringing it up here.

The coaching leader realises the real value of reflection. In a coaching conversation, the leader can and should create the space, where he gives his employee the time to reflect on his tasks, challenges and situations from every angle. Some find it awkward to step back and be reflective when the environment requires action, but on the way from **A** to **B**, it's always more efficient to define the purpose of the journey first.

Emotional Leverage

Pain and gain, two ways to create emotional leverage.

There is no one-size-fits-all best-practice method when it comes to the exploration phase. In the opening phase, together with your co-worker, you decided on the goal of the conversation, the best possible outcome. Now it's your turn to pick and choose the most relevant tools to achieve that result. Where to begin and where to take it from there, is entirely depending on each situation. The tools you use for a 90-minute session around overall performance, are different from those for a 10 minutes session around a single obstacle.

Although you might approach each situation differently, there is one red thread you want to bear in mind during the exploration phase. That is to put emphasis on generating emotional leverage. Emotional leverage is finding out what really is most important to your coachee. Linking to his emotional leverage will help him make a commitment and follow through.

As we already mentioned, there are two opposite forces that motivate people to stick to whatever they've decided: the desire to avoid pain and the desire to gain pleasure. Don't shy away from taking the coaching conversation to the emotional level. The more emotional leverage you manage to 'link' to the coaching-topic, the higher the chances that your coachee will succeed. Pretty basic, but very effective!

Try the Whole Brain approach to create emotional leverage:

- Why is that so important to your team? (R2)
- What positive impact will that have on the bottom line? (L1)
- How can you use your Whole Brain to visualise the best possible outcome? (R1)
- If you fail to implement the changes, how will that affect the overall plan? (L2)

To create awareness and link it to people's emotions is the single most effective way to get people moving. The ground rule in sales is that people buy emotionally, whether it's an object or an idea, and then use logic to justify the purchase. In a coaching session, the coachee is both the seller and the buyer. If the conversation is purely based on logic, the coachee is less likely to follow through with actions than when he's also emotionally attached to the idea.

Resistance to Change

Regardless of the situation, the outcome of a coaching process is usually action oriented and therefore likely to lead to change for the coachee. However, the only one who loves change (apart from

R1) is a wet baby. Knowing that, you could (and should) use the coaching session to prepare your coachee for the process that the coaching might lead to.

If the change has a real impact on him, his projects or his environment, then don't be afraid to dive into it. Give the coachee the space to comprehend the magnitude and the reality of the change. Discuss the positive impact it could have for him as well. Ask your coachee for better alternatives, and accommodate him with the opportunity to face his fears and possible obstacles of the unknown. Wrap things up in the coaching conversation. If you let your coachee deal with loose ends afterwards, he might easily fade away from the idea that the changing process was a good idea in the first place.

The Whole Brain approach:

- What kind of support does he need to follow through (R2)?
- How will the change affect others (R2)?
- How will the change affect the bottom-line (L1)?
- How will your experience benefit you in the process (L2)?
- What options and possibilities could the change generate (R1)?

Ways to Explore

Step into the future, and let your coachee paint the picture.

The single biggest coaching mistake is to give in to the temptation of 'how' too soon! By entering into actions and objectives, you yank your coachee out of the subjective awareness state, where options and possibilities are being explored and alternatives are being generated, into the objective state. You kill the flow and drag him down to earth in a heartbeat.

The exploration phase is about creating awareness and vision. There are numerous ways to fish for reality. It all depends on the situation and desired outcome of the coaching session. The exploration phase is the heart of the conversation and should last for about 50-70% of the coaching time. One way to get your coachee into the exploration phase, is to ask him to describe the 'perfect world' or the 'ideal situation'. 'What would you look like with all these competencies in place?' 'What would be better?' Challenge him to use the Whole Brain approach to create a vision, what would 'done' look like?

Since people tend to stop their thoughts on the first conscious or subconscious obstacle, they don't dare to dream about the possibilities behind the barriers. They are only able to perceive a small part of their reality, using only their conscious awareness. A good way to get your coachee to create subconscious awareness is to ask him to leave all his challenges behind. Ask him to 'fly over them in time and space', and to imagine himself in the future. He will both consciously and subconsciously, find solutions to overcome the challenges he is facing. 'If everything is possible, what do things look like in X months or X years from now?'

When the coachee has his mind in the future, it's important to keep the dialogue in the present tense. There the subconscious mind cannot discriminate between what he is imagining and the reality. In that moment, also give him the opportunity to create emotional leverage. 'Describe the feeling of the accomplishment! – What does it look like? How does it feel? On the scale from one to ten, how satisfied are you with yourself?' If the answer is seven or below, then ask him how he could reach a nine? Then use your questioning abilities:

- What is missing in the picture?
- Who supported you on the way?

- Who else is positively affected by this new reality?
- Which internal obstacles have you overcome? (don't ask how he overcame them though - remember!)
- Which external obstacles have you overcome?
- How did your core values guide you on your way?

These are some powerful questions that can generate the emotional leverage needed to move people far out of their comfort zone, and towards accomplishments they have never even dreamed of before. Now the big question remains, do you have the courage as a leader to take your co-workers on that journey?

▶ How can you decrease the amount of broken promises to yourself?

▶ How can you include conscious reflection in your daily routine?

▶ How can you create emotional leverage for team members who find themselves stuck in their development?

▶ How can you ensure that you will avoid any discussions about actions and goals in the exploration phase?

Chapter 14 – Activation

Now, we have gone through the why's and who's, it's time to take a look at the how, what, and when! In this chapter, we get the coachee down to action. We'll find the best way to connect the outcome of the exploration phase back to reality.

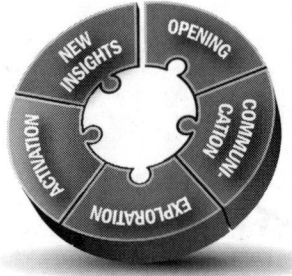

At the end of the exploration phase, you can switch over to activation phase in one question: 'Now that you have described the ideal situation, with the best possible outcome, can you take me through the process of how you plan to get there, step-by-step?'

In this stage, we capture the dynamics of the situation, and gently push the coachee to the edge of his comfort zone. If you have had an effective coaching session, the coachee has probably revealed all the right reasons to fold up his sleeves and get down to action. The momentum should be captured, and documented by an action oriented plan to follow through.

In this phase, you also have the opportunity to challenge your coachee. If your coachee thinks that X is a good number to reach, ask him what XX looks like? What is the difference? What needs to happen to reach that number? Don't push him away; be firm but gentle. After all, it is a change process he is about to step into.

Goal-setting Culture

Within the corporate world, the concept of goal setting is underappreciated for its actual value. It's our impression that goals are used (or misused) to identify how many hours people have to put in to get their bonus, or what they have to do to meet the expectations of the organisation.

Organisational goals are often misaligned with the talent management process. After a coaching session, you should approach the goal setting process differently. Activation shouldn't be about carrots and sticks; it should all be about the coachee, his development, and his way forward.

However, in order to be able to guide your people, and reap the benefits of the goal setting process, you need to first master the art yourself. You need to taste your own medicine, find your drive, and write down your goals. Well, let's see. In this book, there are assignments in every chapter. Have you finished them? Have you taken the time to reflect on, and evaluate, the questions? Have you written down the answers? If you have a clear conscience, well done, good job, congratulations! If not, you probably don't realise the power of writing things down (yet).

The Power of Writing Things Down

Writing things down, for example, goals, thoughts or your daily tasks, can clear your mind for more high-level thinking. David Allen (2001), the author of *Getting Things Done*, recommends doing what he calls a 'core dump'. It involves writing down everything you need to address. Writing down every 'to-do' item you can think of, clears space in your head for more important topics.

Your memory is like a leaking bucket. Writing things down gives you a better overview, and a sense of control. It also gives you the opportunity to clear your mind and collect your thoughts. With

VUCA, we sometimes have our minds filled with information, and all kinds of 'stuff' we are barely able to sort and work through. Setting aside some time to write things down, gives you a better overview of your situation. It's like being in the eye of the storm. It also helps you to process your emotions and challenges. By writing about them, you will see them in a different light, and often discover ways towards more sensible solutions.

Writing things down informs your brain that you intend to honour them.

Mistakes in Goal Setting

You don't make these mistakes, do you?

Of all the mistakes you can make in goal-setting, the biggest one is not having any at all. Some other common mistakes are:

- The decisions and goals are not written down.
- There are conflicting interests between your roles (cognitive dissonance).
- Having too many goals.
- They are not action oriented.
- They are not measurable.
- They are not meaningful.
- They are not thought through.
- They are not realistic.
- They are not set by you.

In our opinion, however, the three major mistakes people make when they are setting their goals, are:

1. They lack clarity and vision.
2. They lack emotional leverage.
3. They are within their comfort zone.

Countless books and websites identify clarity and vision to be the most important parts of the goal setting process. Well, you just took your coachee through the exploration part. You have explored the best possible outcome, various alternatives and the positive impact. **Check**!

Your coachee should also have discovered all the WIIFM's (what's in it for me?) and therefore have emotional leverage attached to the solution. **Check**!

People are often blinded or limited by their idea of how much they can accomplish. There is usually a big gap between where they are and where they could, or want to, be. Most of the time people are working and delivering within their comfort zone. But the greatest difference between a great job and an excellent job is the state of mind. One of the very best ways to enter into, and positively affect, the coachee's state of mind, is through coaching.

With clarity, vision, emotional leverage and all the benefits out on the table, people can do more, and reach further, than they thought they could. No one experiences growth within his comfort zone, so don't be afraid to challenge your coachee to take an extra step, to reach a little further or fly a little higher.

BE-SMART

There's something missing in SMART...

You have probably heard about the SMART way of setting your goals. We don't think it's that smart at all. It's only half of the story, only a left brain activity. Therefore, we like to BE-SMART about it. Being smart is about creating peace between the head and the heart, following your heart and using your head to pave the way. BE is the acronym for benefits and emotional leverage. The BE-part is connected to the WHY and WHO, whereas the SMART-part is connected to the HOW, WHAT, and WHEN. You have probably heard that if you have a big enough WHY; you will find out the HOW and WHAT! It doesn't work the other way around.

That is why it's necessary to BE SMART when it comes to the goal setting process. The acronym SMART is the most popular, but has some variations. They can be used to provide a more comprehensive definition for goal setting.

- **B**enefits (WIIFM)
- **E**motional leverage
- **S**pecific, **s**ignificant, **s**tretching
- **M**easurable, **m**eaningful, **m**otivational
- **A**ction oriented, **a**greed upon, **a**ttainable, **a**chievable, **a**cceptable
- **R**elevant, **r**ealistic, **r**easonable, **r**ewarding, **r**esults oriented
- **T**ime bound and **t**rackable

The Whole Brain Approach

BE-SMART and use the Whole Brain.

We are not going through the specifics of each part of the 'BE SMART' here, since we believe you have already been there and done that. We want to introduce the Whole Brain approach as an alternative, and we challenge you to do the same after each coaching session, to help you implement Whole Brain thinking into your organisation.

When you get to the activation phase in your coaching session you should address the four quadrants of the brain, and find a balance between them. What your coachee sees as most important, often depends on his brain preferences, which may be totally different from yours.

If you are L1, you first want to look at the facts, gain clarity, and hold on to reality. Traceability is one of your main issues. If you are L2, you will put most of your energy into planning and preparation, timing each step of the way. If you are R1, you probably want to try something new, out of the box, 'have fun while you do it'. If you are R2, you will emphasise on agreement, meaningfulness and the effect the goals have on you and the people around you. You see how limited each preference is compared to the Whole Brain approach.

In the Whole Brain approach, you can systematically use powerful questions that lead your coachee through all the quadrants, for example:

- What are the most important facts you need to take into account? (L1)
- How can you analyse various scenarios? (L1)
- What would the perfect plan look like? (L2)
- What are the critical details that need to be sorted out? (L2)
- Which alternative solutions could you benefit from? (R1)
- How could you have more fun on the way? (R1)
- Who has knowledge in this area and might help you to succeed? (R2)
- How will this affect the team? (R2)

Verifying Your Decisions (Goals)

Let's be honest here. Talking about goals in the corporate world is like talking about push-ups or 'the plank'. Everybody knows the benefits but it can be hard to get oneself to stick to the activities. Three minutes of push-ups and a two minute plank each day will have a huge impact on your body in only a few weeks. The same goes for five minutes on your goals each day.

Call them what you want, goals, dreams, decisions, dollies. It really doesn't matter as long as they are given the attention they deserve. Everything you focus your attention on will grow and prosper.

To maximise the effect of a coaching session, the coachee needs time to reflect on, and evaluate, the quality of his decisions (goals). The time needed depends on the length and the content of the session. For a short session on a specific issue, a decision can be made without any writing or formalities. After a longer session, or if the content includes a complex intervention or long-term goal, you might even consider to give him a home assignment and to get back to you with his goals and decisions.

The Action Steps (5 × 5)

If no action is taken, nothing will happen!

At this point in the coaching session, all the groundwork is ready. It's like gardening. You have prepared the soil with fertiliser, the moisture level is perfect and in the exploration phase the coachee has chosen the flowers and seeds. The only thing left to do is to bed and sow—take the first steps and put it into action.

The 5 × 5 is the most efficient action kicker we know. You can play with it as you want, depending on each situation. It really drives people to action, and is only performed with questions. This is how it works, challenge your coachee with the following questions:

- What will happen in the next five minutes?
- What will have happened in the next five hours?
- What actions will you have taken in the next five days?
- What is the impact of your decision (goal) in the next five weeks?
- What will have happened in the next five months?

The answers you get from the questions above are the unpolished diamonds of your coaching session and the groundwork for the last step of the OCEAN coaching model, the New Insights.

▶ Which 'fuzzy' goals that are now on your to-do list could you improve by applying BE-SMART?

▶ How can you coach your team towards Whole Brain Leadership?

▶ What are your 5×5 action steps?

▶ How will you make sure that coachees 'own' their goals?

▶ How will you adjust the goal setting approach to the thinking preferences?

Chapter 15 - New Insights

How do you increase the coachee's self-discipline and help him to follow through and execute? Your coachee has been 'writing a new script'. Now it's time to do the final editing. We have all tasted the bitter fruit of procrastination, of not following through and the erosive effect it has on one's self-respect.

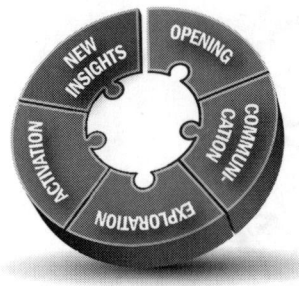

Have you ever experienced the feeling after a meeting, that you were not quite sure if a decision had been taken? Have you ever been held accountable for something you weren't even aware of that it was your responsibility? Most of us have. As a coaching leader, you should never let your coachee leave before you have done a 'New Insights' check. Make sure that it is crystal clear what needs to be done, why it needs to be done, when it's supposed to be finished.

As we have already been through a couple of times, coaching is a conversation where you 'cut the crap', 'get to the core' and 'bridge the gap' between the coachee's words and actions. At the end of each session, the coach has a valuable opportunity to adjust the coachee's behaviours and actions, based on the results of the coaching process, his goals, and decisions.

Zooming Out

One of the ways to perform a reality check, and to ensure a mutual understanding, is to take a mental 'helicopter view' of the session, to affirm the highlights. We usually ask the coachee to take us through this process. A question like 'What new insights have you gathered (or learned) today?' is powerful at this moment, because it increases the coachee's awareness once again. You can also take him through the process yourself to show empathy, and that you have truly been listening. Sometimes the coachee is too involved in the details that he loses the connection with the big picture. There is really no right or wrong here, as long as you zoom out on the conversation in the end.

> *Step into your helicopter and collect your insights.*

Let's try it out and take a quick helicopter view at the OCEAN model:

> In the opening phase, you established the groundwork and created the atmosphere where you could connect with your coachee on a deeper level. You helped your coachee to identify the main issue, the core of the conversation.
>
> You used your communication skills to dive under the surface of the matter, consciously and unconsciously increasing the coachee's awareness and understanding. With powerful questions, you helped the coachee to find ways to overcome his challenges and/or limitations. You then supported him to link emotional leverage to his solutions and got him to establish goals and an execution plan to follow through.

A helicopter view also gives you an insight in your coachee's brain preference.

- Is he exited about the new opportunities (R1)?
- Is he happy about the effect his intentions have on others (R2)?
- Is he looking forward to do the planning (L2)?
- Does he need to do some more research before making the final decision (L1)?

After a good coaching session, the coachee should realise that the status quo is not an option anymore. Some changes are necessary to ensure further development and success.

Resisting Change

Your coachee still considers the upcoming events as a change process. Therefore he may (will) experience feelings of resistance.

In order to survive VUCA, almost everyone agrees that continuous change and adaptation are inevitable. What change means, differs from industry to industry. In general, the need for change is probably one of the few things that is never going to change.

The leader who has the qualities to coach his people through change, is more likely to succeed, both in the short and the long run. You need to realise that, and understand why, people resist change, so you can consciously support them to overcome the obstacles directly linked to the change process.

Referring to the 'Typology of Change' model from Nadler and Tushman (1995), there is a big difference between an incremental change and transformational change. Incremental change is where fine tuning or adaptation is needed to do things better. Transformational change is about doing things completely different, or doing different things. The higher the intensity of the change, the more coaching is needed.

> *Resistance to change is natural. Does that mean you shouldn't change?*

Here are few of the major reasons for resistance and how you can overcome them.

- **The fear of the unknown.** The only one embracing change is R1, with his need for variety and excitement. L1 needs evidence that it will work, the facts to support it. L2 needs a solid plan to enter into the unknown territory, and R2 wants to know that he will have the support from his team and that people won't get indignant on the way.

- **Lack of competence.** The challenge here is that this is an issue people seldom disclose. You need to ensure that your coachee truly beliefs that he is able to meet the challenges ahead. Just throw in a powerful question to create awareness around the subject. 'What competences would you have to work on to ensure your success?' This is a classic whole-brainer. For example, an L1 is likely to be concerned about not having sufficient analytical skills for the job, when he should be focusing on his communication skills and intrapersonal intelligence. An L2 is likely to be concerned about trajectories, and his planning ability, when he should be focusing more on his ability to think out of the box. Get the picture?

- **Re-wiring.** People are hard wired to the old-way of doing things. This is most visible with people having their dominant thinking preferences in L2. By coaching people to change, you are setting yourself up against all the hard-wiring with all the emotional connections linked to them. This is an issue that should be addressed in the Exploration phase and readdressed in the New Insights phase. What are the pros and cons of the old and the new way? If you don't use the opportunity in the coaching session to address the coachee's benefits of the change, you risk that the coachee will stick to the old way because it's so much easier. Again you should use your insights in thinking preferences to speak the coachee's 'language'.

New thinking needs new wiring. Some old wires become obsolete.

- **Lack of motivation.** Compliance is not the same as acceptance. People can be overwhelmed by change. Their body is in, but their hearts are absent. This is a matter of emotional leverage. If you manage to link emotions to the benefits of changing, you have a higher chance of implementing the change successfully. The benefits need to be seen as adequate for all the trouble involved. Remember that the benefits come in different packages, depending on your coachee's brain preference. For L1, the benefits should be logical. For L2, they come in the form of security. R1 is looking for diverseness, while R2 wants to see people grow.

With three large generations at the work floor (baby boomers, Generation X and Generation Y), the variation in how change will be perceived is big. The reaction to change will therefore differ as well. You can imagine that the older generations will challenge the need for change more than the millennials. The older generations have probably experienced several change programmes, most of which haven't been that successful. They may have developed a cynical approach towards change. Millennials, on the other hand, are relatively new in business and consider learning and professional development as top priorities. They understand that change is needed to achieve that.

Our OCEAN coaching model can also be compared to Lewin's three step model of change. He argued that successful change requires a three step process. Unfreeze—Move—Refreeze. 'Unfreezing' in our

OCEAN model is performed in the Exploration phase, 'Moving' can be directly linked with the Activation phase, and 'Refreezing' is the main focus of the New Insights phase. With continuous change at hand, you can argue if 'refreezing' will really happen.

Self-discipline

Successful people often enforce their success with discipline. Our experience has taught us that the right point of bringing self-discipline into the discussion is in the New Insights phase. Let's face it, the single biggest reason for people failing to follow their words with actions, is the lack of self-discipline, their ability to do the things that need to be done.

Bringing up the issue of self-discipline is tricky and often needs to be handled with care. Therefore, we often focus on some of the aspects that are reflected by self-discipline, for example, being focused, being productive, not giving up and respecting deadlines. It all boils down to holding the coachee accountable for what he says he is going to do.

Implementation and Follow-up

We are almost there! The last step, before you finish, is to make sure your coachee has a detailed plan on how he is going to execute his actions and goals. If the change is incremental, minor adjustments to make things a little better or more efficient, a written plan is probably not needed. On the other hand, if the change is transformational, effort and time should be invested in writing down an implementation plan.

An implementation plan is an action-oriented plan, in which your coachee follows up on his goals, breaks them down into manageable subgoals, and assigns time frames to them. Let's compare it with new software. It still needs to go through all kinds of bug finding tests before it's launched to the market. The same goes for goals. They might all be set with good intentions, but when they are turned into an execution plan, all kinds of obstacles and flaws are going to be revealed. It's better to face them upfront, than it is to realise mid-river that they had flaws right from the beginning.

If the change is transformational, a good idea would be to plan follow up coaching sessions to support your coachee on his way. During these coaching sessions, again new insights will come to the surface, and adjustments to the original plans may be necessary. That's all part of the process to become adaptive to VUCA.

- ▶ How will you ensure that your coachee doesn't return to his old routines?
- ▶ How will you support your coachee in achieving his goals?

Part 4
Transformation

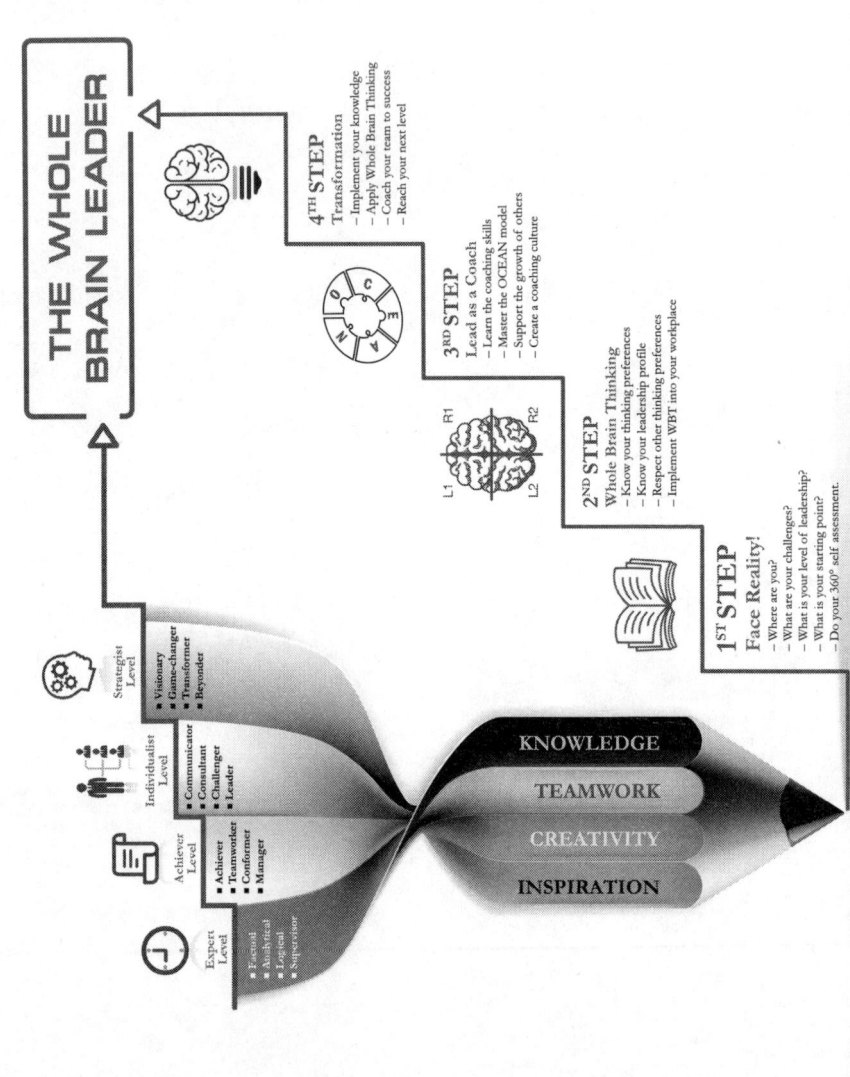

Chapter 16 – Transformation

> *Will you become the transformational Whole Brain Leader, making a huge difference?*

You have reached the defining stage on your journey. You have faced the challenges and reality of leadership in today's business world in Part 1. In Parts 2 and 3, we have showed you two very strong methods to deal with these challenges. Hopefully, you understand that the power of these two methods combined can be transformational. Now the ball is in your court! Are you, or are you not, going to follow through on what you have learned in the previous parts?

Will you become the transformational Whole Brain Leader, making a huge difference? If you want to be part of this select group of leaders, you should make a strong commitment toward yourself and take it all the way, and beyond. We admire your drive and passion for leadership, and look forward to meet you.

However, if you belong to the majority of leaders, that just want to finish the book, without really applying the knowledge, we urge you to think again, and be the change you want to see in others. If you're still not convinced that Whole Brain Leadership will help you to deal with the VUCA world, then please stop reading, because the next chapters are all about taking action, and involve a lot of work. You won't be able to do it, if you're not committed. May we suggest that, when you're not committed to follow through, you give this book to someone else? You may not feel that you can bring about transformation, which we regret, but there are surely others who think they are capable of it, and are willing to take up the gauntlet.

Mark Twain once said, 'Whenever you find yourself on the side of the majority, it is time to pause and reflect'. The majority of leaders today are still stuck in the horizontal development phase, trying to shovel through piles of tasks and projects, doing things right. By now, you certainly realise that some of your major challenges are not in the way 'you do things' (your hard skills), but in 'your way of being' (your soft skills). Generally, your challenges are connected to the development level you're on.

In this chapter, we will do a new reality check, and go through the *why, what, how, who, and when* of the transformation.

Connecting the Dots

As we've discussed, this book should be read, and used, as a kind of travel guide on your development journey towards Whole Brain Leadership. It's now time to reflect on where you are in your vertical development. Remember, we are coaching you now, hence the direct communication. We intend to move you, create action and touch your conscience.

Let's have another reality check. What has happened to your vertical development? If you haven't seriously gone through the exercises, questions and assessments, you haven't moved vertically. If you have engaged yourself in the process, you are heading towards the next level.

If you still find yourself at the expert level, you should now have new insights, and a lot of tools you can use to grow into the independent stage of development. Your challenges lie in developing your interpersonal skills. A solid first step is to do the brain preferences profile. In order to understand how to effectively work with others, you first have to understand yourself. Hard skills alone won't bring you to the next development stage as a leader.

If you have reached the achiever level, you know that understanding how people think is the fundamental skill you need to develop to take yourself, and your organisation, to the next level. You now have the Whole Brain understanding, and the basic know-how to implement coaching into your leadership style, that is, to Lead as a Coach. Further growth will come from applying the methods, and learning from your experiences.

If you find yourself at the individualist level, you don't have to go through any internal negotiations or compromises to realise the synergy you could create. It also makes perfect sense to you to integrate coaching as one of the primary forms of communication. You know that the solutions are already within the people you lead. Further growth will be found in helping others to transform.

When you have successfully taken your organisation through the transformation in Whole Brain Leadership, you may regard yourself to be a strategist.

We are sure you understand that going from expert to strategist is not a matter of just reading a book and going through assignments. It isn't a matter of weeks or months either. For some experts, becoming a strategist will never happen. Each step on the Vertical Development Ladder requires an expansion of the mindset, and therefore time and effort. You have to challenge your assumptions in each stage of your development.

If you reach the strategist level and look back at your development, the transformations you have gone through make perfect sense. When you're at the beginning of your journey, you are about to discover many new things about you and your leadership. From now on, we assume that you have gone through the assignments and developed yourself along the way.

The Need for Transformation

What does transformation mean in your situation?

We appreciate that our readers have different backgrounds, work for different organisations, at different leadership levels, in different industries, live in different countries, experience different levels of VUCA, and so on. Your situation is unique, and only you can estimate the time and effort you need to invest to reach the next level of development.

You have to discover for yourself, what the transformation implies in your case. Let's apply some Whole Brain Thinking and discover the *why, what, how, and who*. In the end, we will also add a *when* to the four leading questions.

Why Should You Transform?

Although we've addressed the issue of change before, we need to take the discussion up again. Now it's not about your coachee; it's about you and your development, your transformation.

In the first step of John P. Kotter's (1996) eight-step Change Model, he talks about 'Creating Urgency', around the need for change. Luckily for us, we don't need to *create* that urgency; it's already there. VUCA is all around us, it has become a fact of life. It's up to us to deal with it. The world cries out for transformational leaders at all levels! Organisations need to transform in order to survive and thrive in the long run. Organisation charts become obsolete, and organisational structures have become more flexible in order to adapt to their environments. For that, you need to tap into the collective wisdom and power of all employees and other relevant stakeholders.

Regarding your personal development, you might see change as 'nice but not necessary'. If that is the case, we urge you to think again. It indicates that you still have a long way to go. Be a game changer not a victim.

About 2500 years ago, the Greek philosopher Heraclitus stated that 'Change is the only constant'. You can say that nothing has changed, change is still the only constant. As a transformational leader, you should first put the oxygen mask on yourself, before you can help your team. Learn to embrace change yourself, and then lead others through the process.

How About Your Barriers to Change?

Take a close look at your attitude towards change. What is engraved in your belief system?

> *Are the barriers for real, or is your mind playing games?*

In Chapter 9, we've discussed a couple of issues that could stand in the way of change. An inflated ego will try to convince you that you already know-it-all. A deflated ego would easily seed some doubts about your ability to transform into a better, improved version of yourself.

One of the biggest barriers to change, across cultures, genders, and generations, is the devil on your shoulder. He is not your friend, and he loves the comfort zone. He is not your enemy either, and you can't kill him. You can tame and control him with critical thinking and hard work. Don't take him serious, and by all means, do not feed him with negative thoughts!

Can your thinking preferences build barriers to change? Yes they can, but knowing that, you can also use your thinking preferences to break them down.

- As an L1 leader, you need to analyse the facts before taking action. Do a reality check on your barriers to change. What are the real pros and cons about the transformation? What are your assumptions, and how well can you prove them?

- An L2 leader has a natural tendency to resist change. If you have your thinking preferences in L2, ask yourself in full honesty if all variables justifying your way of working are still present? Has everything stayed the same, and is your way still the only way to do it right? If you had to start from scratch, how would you design your organisation to deal with VUCA?

- As an R1 leader, you probably don't have objections against change. For you, the challenge will be in the execution. Assemble the right team to go through the transformation, and teach yourself discipline.

- If you are an R2 leader, you may experience anticipated pain of your co-workers. You hesitate to push them through change processes. Use your communication skills to help them to adapt to change as being the only way forward. The VUCA world has no room for the status quo.

The generation you belong to can also form barriers to change. Do you only hang out with like-minded people from your own age, or do you also mingle with other generations? How do you influence each other? What do you bring to the table and which takeaways do you collect? If you want to transform, you need to pick the cherries from all generations, but also be sensitive to feelings of resistance. Get them to the surface and deal with them. Don't allow these feelings to smoulder, because at a later stage they will surely flare up in your face.

What Needs To Be Transformed?

Can you transform your leadership to deal with VUCA?

To be able to deal with VUCA, you have to change and challenge your mindset. The world is changing at an unprecedented pace, and that requires different ways of leadership. As we've discussed in Chapter 1, to deal with **VUCA**, you can use the same acronym.

- **Vision:** Create a clear and shared vision, through individual and group coaching.
- **Understanding:** Create a shared understanding of the context. Share your knowledge and engage people, through Whole Brain Thinking and coaching.
- **Clarity:** Make things simple and clear. Use your Whole Brain to communicate the context.
- **Adaptability:** Take the stiffness out of the organisation. Prepare yourself and others to adapt to VUCA.

The challenges of VUCA are huge, and cannot be solved by just one or a few persons in the organisation. VUCA is here to stay, and it requires new ways of thinking and vertical leaders to pave the way. Leaders that can adapt, and tap into the collaborative powers of those they work with. You have to start with yourself, but you also have to scale up quickly in order to create momentum for the transformation process.

How to Transform?

In Part 1, you did a 360° self-assessment. Now it's time to revisit the assessment, to find out what has changed, and where further development is necessary. You will find the 360° self-assessment in the Appendix, but you can download it from our website as well. You can get an even better overview by asking the people around you to evaluate you as well.

- Where do you need to develop further?
- What has been your greatest victory so far?
- How can you coach others with your findings?

Growth Opportunities

A large part of coaching is visualising the future, and that is a part of the exercise we would like to lead you through.

This is the scenario:

> You are looking back from the future, one year from now. You have implemented your new skillset with great success. You have coached the people around you, and you see the positive impact it has on both the individuals, as well as on the organisation or department as a whole. You have more time on your hands to reflect, and to focus on the strategic part of the business. Whole Brain Thinking has become part of the organisation's culture, resulting in increased productivity and higher engagement.

You haven't crossed the finish line yet! You still need to implement the skills to incarnate the changes as envisioned in the above exercise. How can you apply the knowledge you acquired in the first three parts of the book? Take a look at the opportunities your new skillset could create for you. For each area of 360° assessment, write down your growth opportunities. This assignment is crucial. It has to do with your motivation to change. When you realise the growth opportunities you are facing, you cannot wait to start implementing.

Integrity and Ethical Management	
How will Whole Brain Thinking improve my ability to work ethically according to professional values?	
How will Leading as a Coach improve my ability to work ethically according to professional values?	

Communication	
How will Whole Brain Thinking improve my ability to give and gather information, and to effectively manage the communication process within my organisation?	
How will Leading as a Coach improve my ability to give and gather information, and to effectively manage the communication process within my organisation?	
Motivation	
How will Whole Brain Thinking improve my ability to support and encourage others?	
How will Leading as a Coach improve my ability to support and encourage others?	
Developing Others	
How will Whole Brain Thinking increase my effectiveness in training and the development of individuals and teams?	
How will Leading as a Coach increase my effectiveness in training and the development of individuals and teams?	

(Continued)

Developing Self	
How will Whole Brain Thinking improve my ability to focus on my personal development?	
How will Leading as a Coach improve my ability to focus on my personal development?	
Relationship Building	
How will Whole Brain Thinking improve my ability to get on well with others, and build long-term trusting relationships?	
How will Leading as a Coach improve my ability to get on well with others, and build long-term trusting relationships?	
Teamwork	
How will Whole Brain Thinking improve my ability to contribute to teams and to improve their effectiveness?	
How will Leading as a Coach improve my ability to contribute to teams and to improve their effectiveness?	
Adaptability	
How will Whole Brain Thinking improve my ability to respond and adapt to changing circumstances and to manage in a climate of uncertainty?	

How will Leading as a Coach improve my ability to respond and adapt to changing circumstances and to manage in a climate of uncertainty?	
Influencing	
How will Whole Brain Thinking improve my ability to influence?	
How will Leading as a Coach improve my ability to influence?	
Leadership and Inspiring Others	
How will Whole Brain Thinking improve my ability to use my personal skills to guide and inspire others?	
How will Leading as a Coach improve my ability to use my personal skills to guide and inspire others?	
Creative Thinking	
How will Whole Brain Thinking improve my ability to generate new ideas?	
How will Leading as a Coach improve my ability to generate new ideas?	

If you are anything like the majority of our clients, in some areas you felt confident, whereas in others you probably had to leave your comfort zone. Where did you want to skip the answers or had problems answering the questions? What does that tell you? Why did some areas challenge you more than others?

When you have completed your Growth Opportunities Survey, make sure that you share your findings and make them visual in your office. Let people discuss the findings with you. Your openness will certainly inspire others to find out more about your journey. What an opportunity to get new travellers on board!

Who Needs Transformation?

Will you make a difference? Is it your stone that ripples the water?

You don't really have to answer this! By now, it must be clear that the whole organisation needs to change, but it has to start with you! No matter where you stand in the hierarchical system of your organisation, you can make the difference! It's the level of leadership you possess, not the functional title on your desk or your door.

Just knowing gets you nowhere. It's action that counts!

- What are you going to DO to make the transformation happen?
- Will you really follow up on your growth opportunities or do you take them for granted? What will keep you going?
- How will you handle resistance?
- What will you do with the people that disagree with you on the necessity of the transformation?
- It's a long and bumpy road, do you have the drive and endurance to keep on going?

What Do You Need?

Right now we can imagine that you feel overwhelmed. Starting up the transformational journey, and keep the process towards Whole

Brain Leadership going, is a huge task. We can think of three possible scenarios for you:

- **You dive in head first.** You have the confidence that you can handle this. You believe in yourself and in your organisation. You see the power of Whole Brain Thinking and Leading as a Coach, and know how to apply the newly acquired knowledge. Great! Please continue. If you have any questions, don't hesitate to contact us.

- **You throw in the towel.** For you it's all too overwhelming. There is so much to be done, and you simply don't know where to start. You doubt if you've developed yourself enough (in a vertical way) to get something this big up and running. That would be a pity. You have come this far, and should continue. Maybe the next scenario is something for you.

You're not alone!

- **You call for help.** If you don't have the time or lack the faith or motivation to do it on your own, but you see the need for transformation in your organisation, you can always call in the professionals. We are more than willing to help you set up your transformation process, and help you to execute the plans. We have what it takes to help you getting ready to deal with the VUCA world. Where we don't have the know-**how**, we can rely on our know **who**. We are highly adaptable to your specific circumstances.

When to Start?

Whatever scenario you want to pick, right now is probably the best time to take yourself (and others) to the next level. You have the facts, you have the framework, and you have learned pretty remarkable ways to develop. On top of that, you can also call us for further assistance.

There are no excuses for further hesitance. The VUCA world doesn't wait for your ideal circumstances; tomorrow there will be new excuses.

- ▶ Which obstacles can you think of that may prevent you from starting the transformation process? Write down as many as you can.
- ▶ Which of these obstacles have a high probability to actually occur?
- ▶ Which solutions can you think of to avoid these obstacles?
- ▶ If these obstacles—despite your efforts—still appear, how will you minimise their influence?

Chapter 17 – Become a Whole Brain Leader

Throughout this book, we have prepared you for this final step, to become the Whole Brain Leader! Now we want to challenge you even further. We urge you to look at the opportunities that you can create within your organisation. Although we shift the focus from you to the organisation, it's still you that has to initiate the movement. By teaching and coaching within your organisation, and challenging your coachees to do the same, you can create momentum.

The VUCA world is not only hazardous, it's full of opportunities as well—opportunities that you could miss out on if you don't transform your organisation into an adaptive system, one where leaders coach and people are constantly adapting and aligning. You will gain new insights from the ones you coach to coach, and that will challenge and expand your mindset. You will get buy in when people experience positive changes, and appreciation for who they are and how they work. The seeds of change you've planted will grow, break through the surface, and slowly but surely shape a new and adaptive organisation.

Grow by Sharing

Knowledge is power, but nothing beats sharing knowledge!

In a perfect world, you might be able to visualise that you could even roll out the methods you have learned, on a larger scale. Leadership can then truly become a process, instead of a function.

It's going to be game changing (after all, you are aiming to change the company culture), and therefore it will need a great deal of your attention. It won't be easy, and you must expect, at least some, resistance. The intensity of the resistance depends on the impact the people experience. For some it will be huge, for others minimal. Use your knowledge of, and experience with, Whole Brain Leadership, to reduce the intensity.

Through the years, we have experienced the positive impact from coaching and Whole Brain Thinking within numerous organisations. The majority of leaders involved have successfully implemented either one or both of these methods. People tend to find it interesting to learn more about how they and others think, and are willing to help others when they can apply their thinking preferences to the problem the other is struggling with. Most Whole Brain organisations became more agile due to more value-adding communications and greater respect for the diverseness of people.

By creating new coaches within your organisation, you will create a growing network of Whole Brain Leaders, all with their unique strengths. Can you picture the power of such a growing network, adapting to the demands and opportunities of the VUCA world?

To help you with the practical aspect of things, we have some supporting material that you can download from our website. You are welcome to use it if you want to present the development journey to your team or organisation, or make your own training programme from the book.

Learn by Coaching

Both coach and coachee are in a learning process.

Once you start the coaching journey, you will begin to experience changes around you, and—more importantly—within yourself.

People will start to open up, speak more freely about their ideas, concerns and challenges. They will probably start seeking your coaching support, knowing they will not be judged, but empowered.

It takes courage to become a coaching leader. You may find yourself in a situation you are not comfortable with in the beginning. Just remember that all the answers lie within the ones you coach. You just need to help them dig for their solutions. From experience, we can inform you that although the learning is largely with the coachee, you are also reflecting and learning about yourself. In every single coaching session, you will deepen your level of understanding of human behaviour. You will develop your insights and your sixth sense. That knowledge will come in handy in the long run, because the difference between a good leader and an exceptional leader lies in the ability to sense what can't be seen, and hear what hasn´t been told.

Give yourself the time to reflect on what you learn. The different insights and viewpoints you experience while coaching will prove to be diamonds in the collective learning process. Share what can be shared without ever breaking any form of confidentiality and build on the organisation's collaborative Whole Brain. The more openness, clarity, and sharing you can establish, the more adaptive your organisation will become.

Establish Powerful and Open Networks

It may very well be that the ones resisting change the most, are the ones that fear they will lose their leadership title, those with a hierarchical mindset, most probably working at an expert leadership level or lower. Help them to comprehend that their expertise is still needed, but combined with strengths of others, their expertise increases in value. Explain what synergy means and how this transformation programme will give birth to a system that sparks synergy all around them.

Coach them in such a way that they experience that their gains will make their pains shrink. At first you may need to connect them to others in order to experience the synergy. At a later stage, they will find their ways themselves, and establish powerful and open networks naturally.

Powerful and open networks are highly adaptive. Connections can be opened and closed, depending on the demands and opportunities at hand. The better the people in the network understand each other's thinking and each other's strengths and limitations, the easier they find it to expand their network and the more powerful these networks will grow. When they realise that different demands require different talents, they will not object to continuously build new and close down old networks.

Harness the Power of Trust

If there's no trust, there will be no transformation.

Trust is without a doubt the most important ingredient in the whole transformation process. You can have the greatest visions, goals, plans, and programmes, but if trust has left the building, you're doomed before you start. We have discussed what trust means in coaching (Chapter 11) and showed you how to build trust and trustworthiness as a coaching leader.

Since trust is such a vital ingredient, we would also like to refer to Stephen M.R. Covey's (2008) book, *The Speed of Trust*. It's one of those books each leader should read as a part of his development journey. Covey distinguishes five levels where trust plays its role, these levels are:

- Self-trust
- Relationship trust
- Organisational trust

- Market trust
- Societal trust

He uses the metaphor of Five Waves of Trust to explain how trust expands from inside out, where one is the prerequisite for the next. Your role as a leader is to create and spread trust. For that, you both need to work on your character (expressed in integrity and intent) and competence (expressed in capabilities and results).

When you will create and roll out such an important transformation programme within your organisation, we cannot emphasise enough that a culture of trust is, by far, the most important prerequisite of all. If it's not there yet, you should seriously consider to give it the highest priority. It goes beyond the scope of this book to describe that process. We gladly refer to Stephen Covey's (2008) book and are also more than willing to offer our coaching to assist you in the process.

Leveraging the Power of Generations

Each generation has its pros and cons, just as with thinking preferences. Don't label people as a member of this or that generation. Keep treating them as humans with their own unique qualities. Create synergy to leverage the power of generations. The better you learn to understand the differences between the generations in the organisation, the stronger networks you can create to deal with VUCA.

Connecting the Dots

We are at the end of what we wanted to share with you on Whole Brain Leadership and what it can do to help you and your organisation thrive in a VUCA world. We truly hope you will apply your new knowledge and wisdom to make the transformation a reality, for your sake and for the ones you lead. It will take you to your next level.

People will be tempted to stick to what once was. Unfortunately for them, the world doesn't stop. The VUCA world won't show mercy for the unprepared nor the status quo. You don't have a choice—it's either to adapt or to fade away. If you need help, don't hesitate. Call for help!

We have prepared additional material for you on our website. Feel free to use what you need, but please share your experiences with us. Your stories are very important to us.

Have a wonderful transformation!

- When and where will you start rolling out your programme?
- Who will be involved initially?
- How will you capture your lessons learnt during the programme?
- What does 'finished' look like?

Appendix – 360° Self-Assessment

With the 360° Self-Assessment, you can rate your level of development in 11 different areas by answering five questions per area. First, take the assessment yourself, and after that, you can get an even better overview by asking your colleagues (your boss, subordinates and peers) to assess you as well. If the level of trust is high, you could learn a great deal by having an honest discussion on your areas of improvement. Take your time to fill in the assessment, and revisit the assessment on a regular basis, especially when major changes have occurred.

Integrity and Ethical Management

- My ability to work ethically according to professional values

1. I accept total responsibility for my work and decisions.
2. I admit my mistakes and wrongdoings.
3. I always give credit to deserving parties and do not take credit for the work of others.
4. I preserve and stick to principles even if short-term commercial advantage is compromised.
5. I use positional and personal power with care.

1 - totally agree   5 - totally disagree

Today	Take 2
Q1 1 2 3 4 5	1 2 3 4 5
Q2 1 2 3 4 5	1 2 3 4 5
Q3 1 2 3 4 5	1 2 3 4 5
Q4 1 2 3 4 5	1 2 3 4 5
Q5 1 2 3 4 5	1 2 3 4 5

Communication

- My ability to give and gather information and to actively manage the communication process

6. I ask questions to find the real views of others and check for understanding.
7. I can convey complex information in everyday language.
8. I have a style and presence that makes a positive impression.
9. I listen to, and consider, other views.
10. I use electronic communication channels appropriately, in a way that generates positive reactions.

	Today	Take 2
Q6	1 2 3 4 5	1 2 3 4 5
Q7	1 2 3 4 5	1 2 3 4 5
Q8	1 2 3 4 5	1 2 3 4 5
Q9	1 2 3 4 5	1 2 3 4 5
Q10	1 2 3 4 5	1 2 3 4 5

Motivation

- My ability to support and encourage others

11. I show genuine interest in people and their development.
12. I give praise and open recognition.
13. I have the strength and the maturity to support others through difficulties.
14. I actively involve others and encourage full participation.
15. I motivate others through personal examples.

	Today	Take 2
Q11	1 2 3 4 5	1 2 3 4 5
Q12	1 2 3 4 5	1 2 3 4 5
Q13	1 2 3 4 5	1 2 3 4 5
Q14	1 2 3 4 5	1 2 3 4 5
Q15	1 2 3 4 5	1 2 3 4 5

Developing Others

- My ability to improve performance through training and development of individuals and teams

16. I am able to identify what people are good at and enjoy. I see where they have potential to develop.
17. As a leader, I create a positive learning environment.
18. I inspire others to stretch themselves.
19. I provide personalised coaching and support to others.
20. I understand people's strengths and ambitions, and take them into account when assigning responsibilities.

Today	Take 2
Q16 1 2 3 4 5	❶ ❷ ❸ ❹
Q17 1 2 3 4 5	❶ ❷ ❸ ❹
Q18 1 2 3 4 5	❶ ❷ ❸ ❹
Q19 1 2 3 4 5	❶ ❷ ❸ ❹
Q20 1 2 3 4 5	❶ ❷ ❸ ❹

Developing Self

- My ability to focus on my personal development

21. I seek feedback to support my continuous self-improvement.
22. I evaluate my own performance.
23. I am able to recognise my own development needs.
24. I review and consciously learn from my experience.
25. I take responsibility for my own learning curve.

Today	Take 2
Q21 1 2 3 4 5	❶ ❷ ❸ ❹
Q22 1 2 3 4 5	❶ ❷ ❸ ❹
Q23 1 2 3 4 5	❶ ❷ ❸ ❹
Q24 1 2 3 4 5	❶ ❷ ❸ ❹
Q25 1 2 3 4 5	❶ ❷ ❸ ❹

Relationship Building

- My ability to get on well with others and build long-term trusting relationships

26. I bring tensions to the surface, help to resolve conflicts and produce a positive outcome.
27. I go out of my way to develop trust in my relationships.
28. I am good at resolving people issues before they get out of hand.
29. I am sensitive to the unspoken feelings of others.
30. I do notice when others are in need for help and support.

Today	Take 2
Q26 ① ② ③ ④ ⑤	① ② ③ ④ ⑤
Q27 ① ② ③ ④ ⑤	① ② ③ ④ ⑤
Q28 ① ② ③ ④ ⑤	① ② ③ ④ ⑤
Q29 ① ② ③ ④ ⑤	① ② ③ ④ ⑤
Q30 ① ② ③ ④ ⑤	① ② ③ ④ ⑤

Teamwork

- My ability to contribute to teams and to improve their effectiveness

31. I develop a wide network of productive relationships around the business.
32. I develop ideas and solutions together with others.
33. I encourage a strong sense of team spirit.
34. I give fair and constructive feedback to team members.
35. I actively support, and challenge, less experienced co-workers.

Today	Take 2
Q31 ① ② ③ ④ ⑤	① ② ③ ④ ⑤
Q32 ① ② ③ ④ ⑤	① ② ③ ④ ⑤
Q33 ① ② ③ ④ ⑤	① ② ③ ④ ⑤
Q34 ① ② ③ ④ ⑤	① ② ③ ④ ⑤
Q35 ① ② ③ ④ ⑤	① ② ③ ④ ⑤

Adaptability

- My ability to respond and adapt to change, and to manage in a climate of uncertainty

36. I adopt ideas used effectively elsewhere.
37. I challenge conventional views.
38. I accept beneficial change.
39. I frequently generate innovative ideas and solutions.
40. I easily translate ideas into practical solutions.

Influencing

- My ability to influence

41. I anticipate how others are likely to react and prepare appropriately.
42. I continually evaluate situations and adapt my behaviour accordingly.
43. I have the skills to turn objections into positive outcomes.
44. I am persuasive without being aggressive.
45. I make a strong and positive impact in a group.

Leadership and Inspiring Others

- My ability to use personal skills to guide and inspire others

46. I delegate effectively to others.
47. I know how to generate energy and enthusiasm.
48. I inspire others to believe that they can achieve their goals.
49. I am a source of strength in times of VUCA.
50. I lead without aggression or egoism.

	Today	Take 2
Q46	**1** 2 3 4 5	**1** **2** 3 4 5
Q47	**1** 2 3 4 5	**1** **2** 3 4 5
Q48	**1** 2 3 4 5	**1** **2** 3 4 5
Q49	**1** 2 3 4 5	**1** **2** 3 4 5
Q50	**1** 2 3 4 5	**1** **2** 3 4 5

Creative Thinking

- My ability to generate new ideas

51. I am able to come up with new ways of doing things.
52. I often challenge current thinking to create space for improvement.
53. I am able to make progress by looking at things in a new light.
54. I think 'outside the box' to come up with innovative ideas.
55. I try things out to pursue new and better ways of doing things.

	Today	Take 2
Q51	**1** 2 3 4 5	**1** **2** 3 4 5
Q52	**1** 2 3 4 5	**1** **2** 3 4 5
Q53	**1** 2 3 4 5	**1** **2** 3 4 5
Q54	**1** 2 3 4 5	**1** **2** 3 4 5
Q55	**1** 2 3 4 5	**1** **2** 3 4 5

References

Allen, D. 2001. *Getting Things Done: The Art of Stress-Free Productivity*. Melbourne: Penguin Books.

Covey, S. R. 1990. *The 7 Habits of Highly Effective People, Powerful Lessons in Personal Change*. New York: Simon & Schuster.

———. 2008. *The Speed of Trust: The One Thing That Changes Everything*. New York: Free Press.

de Bono, E. 1985. *Six Thinking Hats: An Essential Approach to Business Management*. New York City: Little, Brown and Company.

Festinger, L. 1957. *A Theory of Cognitive Dissonance*. Stanford, CA: Stanford University Press.

Freud, S. 1923. *Das Ich und das Es*. Leipzig, Vienna, and Zurich: Internationaler Psychoanalytischer Verlag.

Gardner, H. 1983. *Frames of Mind: The Theory of Multiple Intelligences*. New York: Basic Books.

Goleman, D. 1995. *Emotional Intelligence*. New York, NY, England: Bantam Books, Inc.

———. 2006. *Social Intelligence: The New Science of Social Relationships*. New York City: Bantam Books.

Kotter, J. P. 1996. *Leading Change*. Boston: Harvard Business School Press.

McCauley, C. D., W. H. Drath, C. J. Palus, Patricia M. G. O'Connor, and B. A. Baker. 2006. 'The Use of Constructive-Developmental Theory to Advance the Understanding of Leadership'. *The Leadership Quarterly* 17: 634–653.

Nadler, D. A., and M. L. Tushman. 1995. 'Types of Organizational Change: From Incremental Improvement to Discontinuous Transformation'. In *Discontinuous Change: Leading Organizational Transformation*, edited by D. A. Nadler, R. B. Shaw, and A. E. Walton. San Francisco, CA: Jossey-Bass.

Petrides, K. V., and A. Furnham. 2000. 'On the Dimensional Structure of Emotional Intelligence'. *Personality and Individual Differences* 29: 313–20.

Petrie, N. 2014. *Vertical Leadership Development–Part 1: Developing Leaders for a Complex World.* Center for Creative Leadership.

Rooke, D., and W. R. Torbert. April 2005. 'Seven Transformations of Leadership'. *Harvard Business Review.*

Salovey, P., and J. D. Mayer. 1989. 'Emotional Intelligence'. *Imagination, Cognition, and Personality* 9 (3): 185–211.

Starr, J. 2011. *Brilliant Coaching: How to Be a Brilliant Coach in Your Workplace*, 2nd edition. Harlow: Pearson Prentice Hall. [first published 2008]

Whitmore, J. 2009. *Coaching for Performance: GROWing Human Potential and Purpose: The Principles and Practice of Coaching and Leadership*, 4th revised edition. London and Boston: Nicholas Brealey Publishing.

About the Authors

Sjoerd de Waal is the founder of Trainnovation, an innovative training, coaching, and consultancy firm in the Netherlands. He has trained and coached leaders at all levels from Europe to the Middle East. After a career at sea, he spent 20 years in various leadership positions. From this and an MBA from Webster University, he found his passion in Leadership Development. He shares that passion in many ways, such as by writing books and blogs and organising seminars and webinars. In 2014, he published his first book, *Lead Between the Lines*, which was directed at helping first-time leaders to stop suffering, start leading, and get results.

Ingvar Jónsson is a writer, entertainer, and a performance coach within the field of leadership and personal development. He holds a degree in international marketing and an MBA from Copenhagen Business School.

He has built his recent success by training managers and leaders to harness the diverseness of their people by using the LAC (Leader as a Coach) approach together with Neethling Brain Instruments (NBI™). Ingvar is the CEO of Profectus in Iceland and Whole Brain Solutions, the Scandinavian Agency for NBI™.

In December 2017, his latest book, *Your Best Self in 21 Days—For Ordinary People Who Want an Extraordinary Life*, was published in Iceland.

Their paths first crossed in Amsterdam in the fall of 2014, at an NBI™ licensees meeting. It was by pure coincidence that they were sitting next to each other. They discussed their backgrounds; interestingly enough, they discovered that destiny had brought them together. Their walks in life, both personal and professional, were ridiculously similar. They shared the same passion for leadership development, read many of the same books, both finished their MBA at a later stage, both have a background at sea, both have had their share of physical challenges, and both are heading pretty much in the same direction in life. Therefore, it was meant to be that they would go on a journey together.

'This book is a must-read for organizations that are looking to positively engage with the millennial generation. It boldly attempts to define the rules of engagement for a generation that will reshape our future.'

Kiran Mazumdar-Shaw
Chairperson and Managing Director, Biocon

A Fascinating Eye-Opener into the Life of Y!

For special offers on this and other books from SAGE, write to marketing@sagepub.in

Explore our range at
www.sagepub.in

₹495

Paperback
978-93-866-0274-9

'Definitely a masterpiece and a must-have for all business houses and project companies. This is a great book that will not only change a manager's perception about uncertainty but will also provide him/her with many disruptive tools and methods on how to respond to a VUCA situation.'

Tapan Misra
Director, Space Applications Centre, ISRO, Ahmedabad

Master the Art of Dealing with VUCA the Armed Forces Way!

For special offers on this and other books from SAGE, write to marketing@sagepub.in

Explore our range at
www.sagepub.in

₹450

Paperback
978-93-866-0231-2